Sacraments as God's Self Giving

Sacraments as God's Self Giving

SACRAMENTAL PRACTICE AND FAITH

James F. White

with a response by
Edward J. Kilmartin, S. J.

ABINGDON PRESS · NASHVILLE

Sacraments as God's Self Giving

Copyright © 1983 by Abingdon Press

Library of Congress Cataloging in Publication Data

WHITE, JAMES F.
   Sacraments as God's self giving.
   Bibliography: p. Includes index.
   1. Sacraments—Addresses, essays, lectures.
   I. Title.
   BV800.W48   1983   264   83-2659

ISBN 0-687-36707-7

Scripture quotations are from *The New English Bible*, copyright © the Delegates of
the Oxford University Press and the Syndics of the Cambridge University Press,
1961, 1970.

MANUFACTURED BY THE PARTHENON PRESS AT
NASHVILLE, TENNESSEE, UNITED STATES OF AMERICA

To H. Shelton Smith
who taught me the Christian roots
for understanding human rights

Contents ——————————— o

Preface ─────────────────────────── ○

A new reformation of word and sacrament is quietly changing the shape of Protestant worship in America. In contrast to the widely heralded reforms of Post-Vatican II Roman Catholicism, this reformation has made steady progress with little fanfare. Changes in worship are inevitable, as in every other human activity, but frequently such shifts are too subtle and undramatic to provoke widespread notice. But they represent important shifts in the ways Christians understand their relationships to God and to each other. Awareness of such changes and the reasons that underlie them is important in discerning the mind and heart of the Church at any time.

Too often, the Church has been reluctant to think through the witness of its own actions. We have been eager to hear the world speak, to let the world write our agenda, but not apt to listen to our own. The time is ripe for adding new theological priorities to those we now recognize. Someday American Protestantism may see the sacraments as a key for investigations in moral theology, for example. Slowly, very slowly, there are signs of a developing recognition of the centrality of the Church's worship in shaping its witness and mission to the world.

In this book, I encourage Protestants to see and listen to what goes on in the rites and ceremonial of their sacraments. We shall try to understand how early Christians experienced sacraments, beginning with the biblical witnesses to the sacraments' initial impact on the Christian consciousness. We shall reflect on what these experiences now mean for us. We must be willing to go beyond the Reformation of the sixteenth century. No longer can we rest content with the resolution of practices and understandings in that time, any more than Roman Catholics now can be satisfied with that of the Council of Trent. A true catholicism cannot be limited to any century or culture. Our concern here is with reformation in the present, not reformation as past. Hence, I do not

9

hesitate to take the position of an advocate when a tract for the present time seems needed.

To be sure, Protestants can learn much from contemporary Roman Catholic reformers, and the enormous changes they have brought about in sacramental practice and faith. Yet there are enormous riches in the various Protestant traditions that more Protestants would cherish greatly if they were aware of their value. An unstudied tradition is apt to be cast aside with indifference in favor of one that is the subject of much reflection. This is not a matter of respective merits but of the greater appeal that a tradition, which has examined and interpreted its own practice, has over the attractions of an unexamined and uninterpreted one. Though this book advocates many changes, it is also a deeply conservative defense of many practices long familiar yet undervalued.

I call the method I have employed the liturgical circle. We begin the circle by observing what the church says and does in its gatherings for worship. These experiences are considered very significant expressions of the faith of the church. On the basis of such observation, we then move to theological reflection, as to the meaning of the faith thus expressed. We complete the circle by using such reflection as the basis for suggesting worship reforms by which the faith can be expressed in more effective ways. Practice leads to theology, which then returns to practice. We move from experience to seeking understanding to ministry. This liturgical circle, which I earlier applied to the study of the Christian year in *Seasons of the Gospel* (Abingdon Press, 1979), is applied in chapters 2 to 4 in dealing with individual sacraments and in the structure of the book as a whole.

If such a method can be categorized, it is a functional approach. We ask what each sacrament does for the community that utilizes it. We explore what happens in each sacrament and how it can be reformed to serve even better. This method derives theology from sacraments rather than imposing upon the sacraments an abstract theology that fits some better than others, but in which all lie a bit uneasily. I have deliberately changed the sequence of Yngve Brilioth's famous title, *Eucharistic Faith and Practice*, for my subtitle: *Sacramental Practice and Faith*.

Chapters 2 to 4 each begin with a short description of what the church does, and the volume ends with a chapter on the reformation of present practice in the churches. That chapter is especially germane to those in the center of the liturgical spectrum in American Protestantism (Reformed, Methodist, and portions of the Free Church traditions). But it should also be of interest to onlookers from other traditions.

I have intentionally avoided historical study except in rare passages. I believe it is unfair to the reader to repeat material present in my first volume in this Christian Worship in Transition series, *Introduction to Christian Worship* (Abingdon Press, 1980). Those wishing to trace historical developments can find such outlined in that previous volume or in other textbooks on the subject.

It is always a pleasure to pay tribute to those who have made a book possible. The dedication records my deep gratitude to Professor H. Shelton Smith, now in his ninetieth year. His teaching, life, and friendship have helped me experience in my own life the centrality of justice in the Christian way of life. The witness of his own life has been his best teaching method.

I am grateful to Jack Maxwell, president of Austin Presbyterian Seminary, and to the faculty for inviting me to give the E. C. Westervelt Lectures at their annual midwinter convocation. An initial version of the first three chapters was presented as those lectures in February 1981. Subsequent versions were given as the Freitas Lectures at Asbury Seminary in March 1982 and at the Spring Convocation at Eden Theological Seminary in April 1982.

Many men and women have contributed greatly to sharpening my thought through their comments on this manuscript. I am especially happy to recognize thankfully the contributions of Arlo Duba, Richard L. Eslinger, Hoyt L. Hickman, Leroy T. Howe, Paul W. Hoon, Don E. Saliers, Decherd H. Turner, Jr., and Charles M. Wood. Sally Snow has done marvelous work in bringing decency and order out of the wild jungle of my manuscript. I feel obliged to pay tribute to Gustav Mahler, Edward Elgar, Charles Ives, and Aaron Copland whose music gave joy to the writing of so many pages. I hope some of their music lingers in my words.

Other than the intrinsic value of such study for its own sake, justice and ecumenism seem to be the chief extrinsic reasons for the study of Christian worship. Accordingly, I am very appreciative for the ecumenical concern of Edward J. Kilmartin, S.J., expressed in his willingness to contribute the final chapter, "A Roman Catholic Response," to this discussion. Father Kilmartin directs the graduate program in liturgical studies at the University of Notre Dame and is a distinguished scholar of the Christian sacraments.

I am most grateful for the patience of my family for tolerating my absence of mind and body during my days, now ended, of being chained to the typewriter.

June 28, 1982
Passumpsic, Vermont

James F. White

1

The Humanity of the Sacraments

God's self giving is the basis of the Christian sacraments. Throughout the history of the Western cultures, self giving has also been exalted as the noblest form of human expression among pagans and Christians alike. The heroes of Marathon, Horatio at the bridge, the Christian martyrs, and Roland, all provide heroic examples of the most dramatic forms of self giving. Yet, self giving is a daily experience in numerous unspectacular ways for all of us. We give of our time, of our goods, of our feelings to others every day. Each meal we feed a small child is more than food, it is a self giving mediated through feeding.

Self giving is such a common means of human expression that rarely do we think through the diverse forms it takes. Yet it also provides the chief means through which Christians know God whose self giving Christians experience in many ways, but supremely in the Christ event: "God loved the world so much that he gave his only Son" (John 3:16). The Incarnation is the story of God's self giving through becoming one of us. For God's self giving, just like that of human beings, has to take visible or audible form so others may recognize it. The climax of history, as Christians see it, came in those first-century years in which God's self giving took the visible form of a person—Jesus of Nazareth.

But God's self giving continues to be manifest among human beings long after the end of Jesus' historical visibility. The preaching of God's word makes that self giving audible, and the words and actions of sacraments make it both audible and visible. Christians in every age experience anew God's self giving because it is proclaimed and enacted in their midst. They know themselves the reality of God's love as it once was, and now is made audible and visible in Christ.

We shall explore in this chapter the human experience of self giving, which the sacraments reflect through their use of words and actions. We shall also see how sacraments operate in the context of the community of faith known as the Church.

Throughout this book, the motif of self giving will be followed as the most satisfactory thematic element for viewing the use God makes of sacraments. Before we examine the Church's experiences of each sacrament, it is helpful to look at them in general. Though each is unique, our thesis is that all have a common basis in that form of expression known as self giving. The humanity of the sacraments rests on God's use of the same means for expression of self giving as people use. How to understand divine self giving better is our task, and the best approach is to examine the human parallels.

I

It should be no surprise that to speak of God's work we must use human analogies. Both the Old and New Testaments are full of anthropomorphic terms. The "hand of God" is but one of many metaphors that interpret God's will or actions in human terms (examples, I Sam. 5:11; II Chron. 30:12; I Pet. 5:6). Christian theology has long looked on analogy as a necessary tool for discussing God. In recent years, there has been an explosion in our knowledge about our own humanity through research in such human sciences as cultural anthropology, sociology, psychology, and communications theory. This has enormous consequences for our understanding of the ways God relates to humans in the sacraments.[1] It is not strange that we must discuss the sacraments from an anthropological point of view. For, just as surely as they are theological, they are also anthropological.

Thus, we begin by examining more closely one of the key ways through which humans relate to each other, namely self giving, and the various means by which it is expressed. There are obviously many other ways people relate to one another: rivalry, hatred, indifference, exploitation, impatience, and on and on. Self giving is unique in that it involves some means for the giver to surrender a bit of his or her own personal being for the sake of another. Be it as minor as a few minutes of time, or as major as a gift of great value, what is communicated is the willingness to give of one's own being.

Self giving is essentially a means of expressing that kind of love known as *agápe*, the unselfish pouring out of self for the benefit of another, without thought of return. The New Testament uses a variety of words for love, but "the agape group is indeed the most frequent and important for New Testament writers when they speak about love," especially "in the Pauline letters and the Fourth Gospel."[2] Jesus indicated the deepest form of love in terms of self giving: "There is no greater love [agapen] than this, that [someone] should lay down his life for his friends" (John 15:13). This kind of love Jesus not only talked about but personified, by making his whole life and death self giving.

Self giving frequently appears in much less dramatic ways. Someone may ask, "Can you give me a few minutes of your time?" Now, no one can create time or dispense it, but we can give of ourselves by giving our attention to another person for a few minutes. That is what the request really means: One is giving of oneself through giving attention to another. Conversely, when we say we are too busy, we are really saying that we do not wish to give of ourself to someone.

We give or refuse self in many casual ways throughout each day. Calling or writing another person out of friendliness are everyday forms of self giving. Helping a child with homework, washing the dishes with someone, bringing another a cup of coffee, all these are more than just meaningless gestures; they are self-giving signs of love. The refusal to make such gestures is equally significant in evidencing the lack of love that would otherwise find expression in self giving.

At the other extreme are dramatic acts of self giving of heroic character. We call these sacrificial because in them the giving of self surpasses what anyone has a right to expect or demand. Sacrificial giving means giving of an exemplary nature that exceeds all normal expectations. Thus, we cannot expect another to risk life or safety for us though instances abound for such actions. People frequently do surrender their own well-being or lives for the benefit of others as their self giving bears witness to a love that is truly selfless.

Three conditions for self giving can be recognized: the self that is capable of giving, the recipient, and the means of giving. We must discuss these briefly.

One must be a self, distinct from others, in order to give. It is questionable whether a newborn baby, not yet able to distinguish self from non-self, can give anything. But once it begins development as a person, it is able to respond to others, and can respond to affection by smiling. Daily its repertoire of self-giving acts increases. We exist in detachment from others before we can contribute anything to their being. Otherwise, we would just be reshuffling actions within the same organism.

At the same time, we need someone else to give to. We depend on others as objects for our affection. They need not be physically present, but we cannot give ourself without their existence. The lover must have a beloved in order to love. Love is never real in the abstract; there has to be a recipient. Even self giving to a cause is usually to that cause as personified by individuals. We love not the Church as abstraction, but people who make up the Church. Thus, self giving is a means of relating, of bridging selves that exist independently and distinctly from each other. It forms a means through which love can leap across the gulf that separates us from each other.

The third necessity for self giving is a means to express that giving from one independent self to another equally independent self so as to create a new, if only momentary, relationship between giver and recipient. Without some means of expression, that relationship never becomes perceptible. Love must be expressed to be recognized by another. We frequently identify a kiss with love itself. Of course, a kiss is not love, but a means of expressing love. But a kiss can also be perverted into a means of betrayal.

Self giving, as we have said, is the means by which agape love finds expression. Through self giving, love becomes visible, audible, tangible, in short, capable of being perceived by another. Love demands some means of expression, and self giving provides the necessary signs of love.

How do we express love to others? How do we give ourselves away? Our human self giving depends on two means: words and actions. What we say and what we do are frequently combined, but either or both are necessary for self giving to occur and to be recognized. Sometimes these two means are contrasted. Jesus told a parable of two sons (Matt. 21:28-31). One son promised but refused to act; the other refused to promise but did act. In this case, action was obviously the superior means of self giving. But frequently, saying the right words is equally important, as when we need to be told we are loved as well as shown. Both doing and saying are essential. They are how humans give; *we give ourselves through both words and actions.*

Though they usually go together, let us examine first how words provide the means for self giving and then look at actions. The spoken word usually provides our most explicit and concise form of expression. Using words, we can conjure up a vast variety of images within the time span of a few minutes. Think of how many experiences, memories, and ideas can be recalled within a few moments of speech. Rhetoric can combine the most disparate images and construct a totally new reality. Through the spoken word we literally "speak our mind," that is, reveal to another what we are thinking and feeling. We give up our own privacy by inviting another to share in our thoughts. The opposite is also true; refusal to speak is denial to another of access to our own mind and emotions.

Even a casual greeting is, in some minor way, a self giving in which we acknowledge the other's presence and give at least token acknowledgment of the value of that presence. A so-called total stranger is someone to whom we do not accord a sign of recognition. But even that may vary. On a busy city sidewalk we ignore strangers; on a mountain trail they are greeted. Even in such a greeting as a hello, words become a means of self giving as we, in effect, say, "You are part of my world and I am part of yours." This is the minimal exchange and yet initiates further possibilities of self giving.

At times, words are profoundly important vehicles for self giving. At the center of the wedding service are vows in which we literally give ourself to another and take another as spouse through the use of words. [3] On occasions, we use words to make covenants between ourselves and God or to renew such covenants. In a legal context we use words to convey or to receive property through the use of written contracts. Even God's work of creation is described for us in terms of speech: "God said, 'Let there be light,' and there was light" (Gen. 1:3).

Words presuppose a community of meaning we share with others so that speech or writing can be a form of communication. Each word is subject to definition; each syntax has a definite function. Even so, a certain amount of ambiguity is always present. The meaning we intend to give is not always the meaning that is received. Sometimes we give more of ourselves than we expect. A slip of the tongue, a dead giveaway, is an unexpected moment of self-disclosure. Or, at times, we may confuse people so that the self offered is not the self perceived. But generally, our language forms a deliberate and sequential means of sharing ourselves with another or with a group.

The use of spoken words in public worship is central in the life of any Christian community of faith. Even Quakers, who have dispensed with most outward actions, find the spoken word usually essential for their communal worship. The use of spoken words in worship occurs in three different ways. We speak *to God*, we speak *for God*, and we speak *to each other in God's name*. In all these ways, Christians see themselves as responding to God's word spoken in creation and redemption, to which worship is a response

17

and continuation. How is the spoken word used in Christian worship as a means of self giving?

First, Christians *speak to God* most directly in the form of prayer. We give ourselves in various ways through prayer besides the obvious form of offering of self (oblation). We recall before God our concerns and anxieties for ourselves (petition) or for others (intercession). We also remember (offer) before God what Christ has already done on our behalf and beg for the completion of what Christ has promised to do (supplication). We shed our defenses and offer our soiled lives for God's cleansing (confession). We offer thanksgiving through "our sacrifice of praise and thanksgiving" as we recall God's saving acts and express our gratitude and praise for them.

In such speech addressed to the first person of the Trinity, we speak through Christ, and by the power of the Holy Spirit. Christian prayer, ever since the early centuries, has been addressed to the first person through Jesus Christ. And, as Paul indicates, "Through our inarticulate groans the Spirit himself is pleading for us, and God who searches our inmost being knows what the Spirit means, because he pleads for God's own people in God's own way" (Rom. 8:26-27). Within our self giving, through the words of prayer, is also contained God's own self giving. We do not pray alone but through and by God's participation.

In worship, Christians also *speak for God*, just as the Bible speaks of those who speak for another as messengers or heralds. The reading of God's word as found in the scriptures and the interpretation of that word as expounded in the sermon are means by which we speak in God's name. The whole congregation also shares in proclaiming God's word through psalmody and hymnody. Again, ordinary words are spoken, but God uses human words as a means of divine self giving. Biblical faith insists that God uses men and women to speak for God. "I put my words into your mouth" (Jer. 1:9); "I will help both of you to speak" (Exod. 4:15); "Whenever I said, 'I will call him to mind no more, / nor speak in his name again,' / then his word was imprisoned in my body, / like a fire blazing in my heart, / and I was weary with holding it under, / and could endure no more" (Jer. 20:9). Speaking for God is also speech enabled by God's self giving through our words.

At the same time, we *speak words to each other in God's name* as a part of worship. They may be words of greeting, words of forgiveness, words intended to edify and encourage one another's faith, or even the mechanics of spoken rubrics enabling us to do our worship in common. Some of these words may be purely utilitarian; others may be deep means of self giving for "forgiven and reconciled people." Thus, the vertical (human-Godward) dimension of worship is always embedded in the horizontal (human-human) direction. Each worshiper brings different gifts to share with the worshiping community as "the work of one and the same Spirit" (I Cor. 12:11). Even the folksy greeting may be a word in which human self giving is united with God's.

In other terms, our self giving through the means of words in worship is united to God's. The source and object of our words are one. Luther's comment about worship is appropriate, especially if understood in a corporate sense "that nothing else be done in it than that our dear Lord Himself talk to us through His holy Word and that we, in turn, talk to Him in prayer and song of praise."[4] God talks, we talk. In speech we are giving, God is giving, together in a community in which the Holy Spirit dwells. It is ordinary speech made extraordinary by the work of the Holy Spirit. The Christian community cannot long survive unless it experiences the power of ordinary language to unify, to heal, to reconcile, to edify, and to give themselves to one another. Common words gain most uncommon power as they are used in worship.

Words are not the only means humans use to express self giving; actions are also essential. We have a curious saying that actions "speak" louder than words, and, indeed, it often is true that our actions reveal more of ourselves than our words do. The two means of self giving—words and actions—are not in conflict with each other. In most cases they go side by side. It is only when there is a disparity between words and actions that we realize something is amiss. Agreement of our word and our deed is a sign of integrity.

How do we use actions intead of words as a means of self giving? It may vary from the trivial, such as helping in housework as a sign of love, to the ultimate sacrifice. The fullest form of love, as Jesus said, is the giving of one's life for another (John 15:13). Between the most trivial and fullest forms are countless actions through which we give ourselves to others. It may be through play as we give of our time and energy to increase others' enjoyment. Or, work may be a way of helping another by giving of oneself. Through the action, we find a means of expressing our love by making it visible in self giving.

A very significant act of self giving is the giving of a gift. We cannot literally hand ourself over to another, and yet we can do this vicariously through the giving of a gift. We can put our heart in our hands. When we give a gift, we are giving, not just an object, but a sign of ourselves handed over to another for that one's enjoyment or benefit. Part of ourself has been surrendered for another's enhancement. The gift becomes a sign representing the giver. One can say that the gift is the giver since, through the gift, another can receive our will and intention of giving ourself. When we give a gift we do not ordinarily say, "This is my body," or, "This is me," but that is what we mean. And the receiver understands the gift this way, and not merely as an anonymous object. Our homes are full of things we hang onto, not for their usefulness, but because someone we love gave them to us. And to dispose of them would be tantamount to forgetting that person.

We all know people who have a marvelous talent for giving gifts. They know us well enough to know what we need. Often their gifts surprise us, but usually they soon become indispensable because they fit some niche in our lives we never knew was vacant. To give well, one has to know and understand the receiver well. Those who give gifts well succeed in giving themselves to us because their gifts convey so well knowledge of and concern for us.

Actions often provide the most satisfactory form for making love visible or, as the case may be, tangible. Through the use of a variety of actions, love can come into being and grow by expression. It is no accident we call the most intimate form of self giving through sexual intercourse "love." Sex is something that people in love do, rather than discuss at length. The act itself becomes the means through which we express self giving.

Public worship depends constantly on the use of actions as means of expressing God's self giving to us and our self giving to God and to one another. Again, we are not contrasting words and actions. Most of what we do in worship is also accompanied by spoken words. Words and actions—technically rites and ceremonial—complement each other in worship as in life. Some of our actions in worship (like some of the words) are purely utilitarian: we sit for comfort, we announce hymns.

But certain actions we perform together in worship are particularly important bearers of meaning. In recent years it has become common to speak of meaningful actions as sign-acts. Our daily life is full of sign-acts; the handshake is a common one, expressing a form of greeting. Certain sign-acts convey important meaning when performed in the context of a worshiping community. A very select list of these we call sacraments. By no means are all sign-acts sacraments, but all sacraments are actions that convey meaning to represent sign-acts. There are many sign-acts in our worship that are not called sacraments: the offering of money, foot washing, and the gesture of giving a benediction are sign-acts, but not sacraments. The very act of assembling in Christ's name for worship is one of the most important sign-acts of Christian worship, though not a sacrament.[5]

The chief distinction between sacraments and the other sign-acts used in worship is the church's long-standing history of the experience of both God and human beings working in those sign-acts called sacraments. People perform them, but through them experience God's self giving. A human being is not the only actor in these actions. As Luther said: "For man baptizes, and yet does not baptize. He baptizes in that he performs the work of immersing the person to be baptized; he does not baptize, because in so doing he acts not on his own authority but in God's stead. Hence, we ought to receive baptism at human hands just as if Christ himself, indeed, God himself, were baptizing us with his own hands."[6] It is God who really baptizes, though we use the water. Human beings perform the outward action, the visible sacrament; but it is God who acts in self giving to give the inward fruit that makes it a sacrament and not just another sign-act.

Sacraments involve both words and actions. Protestants and Roman Catholics alike have long histories of being all too willing to let words replace much of the action. It is easier to talk about washing than really to do it. Frequently, actions become formalized or replaced by words altogether, until reform makes us aware of recovering the fullness of action, e.g., of giving the cup to the laity instead of just saying the words. Words cannot do it all; neither can actions. Augustine said: "Add the word to the element [action], and there results a sacrament."[7] If anything, it is the actions that have been neglected, not the words. Much of the reform of our times is concerned with overcoming the neglect of meaningful actions. As we explore God's self giving in the sacraments, actions deserve as much attention as words, although the two express the same reality.

If, by words, we speak to each other in God's name, in the sacraments we often *touch each other in God's name*. We act for God in acting to each other. At the heart of several sacraments is the laying on of hands, through which power, blessing, or authority is conveyed. In Mediterranean cultures, it was only natural that olive oil be used as a sign of touching in order to anoint for healing, for initiation, for ordaining. Our worship is full of hands: giving the peace, baptizing, pronouncing benediction, giving the body and blood of the Lord, uniting the hands of lovers, sprinkling a coffin with dust. We touch each other, and we handle bread, a cup,

21

water, and oil. These actions are powerful signs of realities that complement what can be said with words.

But human beings do not act alone in them. These sign-acts are important actions because through them Christians experience God's self giving. Our human actions are needed to give visible form, to make incarnate the divine action. Because our humanity needs actions as outward and visible signs of self giving, God gives us sacraments so that we can know that which is inward and spiritual. It is no different from knowing our neighbor through his or her actions. God gives Godself through actions, too. As with words, the Holy Spirit works through the actions that the Christian community performs in God's name. Thus, when we baptize, our action is experienced as the giving of the Holy Spirit.

II

If words and actions are essential means that all people use for expressing their love to others through self giving, these same means are no less important in God's own expression of love to human beings. God uses the same means of self giving as we do to make God's love known among us.

Christian faith is firmly centered in God's act of incarnation in Jesus Christ. In Jesus Christ the love of God took visible form and lived among us in historical visibility. This act of self giving is the supreme means through which humans know the love of God. "No one has ever seen God; but God's only Son, he who is nearest to the Father's heart, he has made him known" (John 1:18). Because of God's action in incarnation, there can be no doubt as to the sacrificial nature of God's love for human beings. An unknown God is revealed to all people through the Incarnation.

It is in this sense that Edward Schillebeeckx, the Flemish Dominican theologian, can speak of Christ as "the primordial sacrament." He says: "The man Jesus, as the personal visible realization of the divine grace of redemption, is the sacrament, the primordial sacrament."[8] Encounter with Christ becomes the sacrament of our encounter with God. Through him, God acted in incarnate form in the past to make divine love visible even within finite human time and space.

As the primoridal sacrament, Christ is the source of all individual sacraments that carry on what he initiated. Schillebeeckx quotes from a famous Ascension Day sermon of Pope Leo I, "What was visible in Christ has now passed over into the sacraments of the Church."[9] That which God acted out in Jesus

Christ in historical visibility during his years on earth, now, through sacraments, is given to us in our time and place in "earthly visibility and open availability." Christ continues his work, begun in the first century, throughout subsequent centuries. His self giving through sacraments is a constant sign of God's love for us in "outwardly perceptible form."

In Christ, God's love for human beings became visible. Each year, Christians observe the feast of the Epiphany or the Manifestation of God in Jesus Christ. The feast of Baptism of the Lord witnesses to the day on which Christ became manifest to the many. The Fourth Gospel tells us the miracle at the wedding "at Cana-in-Galilee is the first of the signs by which Jesus revealed his glory and led his disciples to believe in him" (2:11). Human love is not the only kind that needs to be made visible. God's love also needs means of manifestation.

To this end, God gives us sacraments as a continual means of manifesting God's love for us. Calvin is emphatic that, since our faith is weak, we need visible signs of God's love. "Our merciful Lord," Calvin tells us, "so tempers himself to our capacity that, . . . he condescends to lead us to himself even by these earthly elements, and to set before us in the flesh a mirror of spiritual blessings."[10] Our Creator knows us best since God, after all, endowed us with such capacities as we have. Thus, we are known even better than we know ourselves. God's way of relating to us reflects the Creator's own knowledge of what it is to be human. Calvin's insight is an important one: God approaches us on our own terms in the sacraments. Through them, God "imparts spiritual things under visible ones." Granted Calvin did not have an overwhelmingly high appreciation of humanity's capacity. The sacraments for him are "visible signs best adapted to our small capacity" through which Christ acts, "by giving guarantees and tokens he makes it [his union with us] as certain for us as if we had seen it with our own eyes."[11] But Calvin is surely correct in understanding the weakness of human faith and our need of manifestations of God's love.

The humanity of the sacraments consists in their accord with human capacities and needs. Just as we have seen how necessary it is for human love to be expressed as self giving for another person to perceive it, so it is equally vital that God's love be expressed by perceptible means. These the sacraments provide as ways through which God accommodates to our capacity in order to make God's love known. Through the words and actions of the sacraments, God reaches out to us in self giving so as to make God's love remembered and experienced anew. Whatever the limits of our capacity for faith, God fits it directly through the proclamation of the word and celebration of sacraments. Through these sign-acts we receive continual signification of God's love. It is no accident that God uses the same means as humans; God, after all, knows us best. We now need to look at the use God makes of words and actions in sacraments.

The concept of "word" has particularly strong meaning for members of the Judeo-Christian tradition. In the Old Testament, the term *dabar* signifies that self giving that occurs in God's word. God speaks and creation occurs. God speaks and it is. God's word goes forth with power. "There shall fall to the earth nothing of the word of the Lord" (II Kings 10:10 RSV). The word creates and gives life, for it is God's chosen form of self expression.

In the New Testament, the term "logos" is used by John to speak of Christ. It has both the power of creation and the power of redemption. "When all things began, the Word already was. . . . All that came to be was alive with his life, and that life was the light of men" (1:1, 4). "The Word became flesh," dwelling among humans, that they might see the glory of God. The Word is the Incarnate One, working within human history.

But the term "word" has a third theological meaning as the word written in scripture, which becomes a present event when encountered through reading and preaching in public worship. Both the written and spoken testimony depend upon the living reality of Christ, which the Holy Spirit enables us to hear and recognize in the context of the worshiping community. Through the working of the Spirit, the past historical work of Christ, and the eternal reality of Christ are both given to us in worship as present event.

Each service of worship becomes a new creation through the proclamation of the word as a means of Christ's self giving afresh. Whenever there is worship in which scripture is read and preached, there is a fresh epiphany, a manifestation of the love of God. Christ "is present in his word, since it is he himself who speaks when the holy scriptures are read in the Church."[12] Christ gives himself to us anew through public reading and preaching just as he did in his first-century incarnation. The same power to salvation is present in our worship as that experienced by the original eyewitnesses.

At their best, all sacraments include, however briefly, some form of proclamation of God's word as experienced through scripture. Recovering this unity of word and sacrament is high on the list of reforms needed in all churches. Word and sacrament are not distinct realities but part of the same event. It is one and the same Christ who is given to us in both preaching and action. The same Spirit makes Christ manifest in both but by different means. Thus, word and sacrament are characterized more by similarity than by diversity. They are never in competition, but each is mutually dependent on the other, reflecting our full humanity.

The reading and preaching of God's word through scripture is especially apparent in the Lord's supper. Luther stressed that "a Christian congregation should never gather without the preaching of God's Word and prayer."[13] Calvin is equally insistent: "the right administering of the sacrament cannot stand apart from the Word, for whatever benefit may come to us from the Supper requires the Word: whether we are to be confirmed in faith, or exercised in confession, or aroused to duty, there is need of preaching."[14] Pulpit and table point to one reality, Christ. When we speak of the eucharist, the term itself includes preaching by definition.

Sacraments include the use of many words besides those used for reading and preaching. As seen already, sacraments include words spoken to God as in prayer, words spoken for God as in proclamation, and words spoken to each other in God's name as in making peace. All these words are part of the sacramental event. We prefer, today, to avoid giving undue emphasis to sacramental formulas as if they create a climactic moment and all else is only preliminary. All the words spoken in worship are used as part of God's self giving. Through them, the Holy Spirit works for the building up of the worshiping community.

Actions are equally important. Protestantism has tended to neglect humanity's need for the visible and tangible, despite Calvin's warning that our humanity demanded such means. We have, instead, settled for a lopsided anthropology, as if words were somehow more spiritual than actions. Who can say that Christ's self giving through bread and wine is any less real than through the words of the sermon? It is the same Christ made known through different means. Our humanity depends upon both words and actions for perception in worship as in everyday life.

The neglect of actions in Protestant worship runs contrary to the biblical witness that shows how important sacraments were to the New Testament church. The centrality of the sacraments in worship persisted until the sixteenth century but was lost to Protestantism despite Calvin's plea that anything less than the eucharist each Sunday was insufficient. The rationalism of some Reformers in the sixteenth century, and of the Enlightenment in the eighteenth, took offense at the idea that physical elements or actions could have any spiritual efficacy. Zwingli wrote in 1525, while defending infant baptism, that "it is clear and indisputable that no external element or action can purify the soul."[15] Such a muted value for actions reflects a distorted view of what it is to be human, as if we give ourselves only through words. The issue is the need for a more adequate anthropology.

Unfortunately it is easier to talk about something than to do it. Too easily we settle for minimal actions. Yet the witness of our humanity is for the need for the fullness of sign-acts both in human relationships and in communion with God. Minimalism is a threat because it negates much of what it means to be human. When we underplay a sacrament, it is the same as mumbling a sermon. In either case, the people are not fed. At many points in life, actions speak when words fail. Going to be present with someone who is seriously ill or recently bereaved is what matters, not saying the right words. Actions are essential when words become inadequate. That is part of being human.

Theologians in recent years have devoted much attention to the fact that sacraments are actions that signify. The traditional statement, as reflected by Aquinas, "that the sacraments of the New Law not only signify, but also cause grace"[16] has usually led in the past to endless discussions of how grace was caused but very little concern with what was signified. Today, however, interest has shifted to the other verb, "signify." This has produced revolutions both in our understanding of the sacraments and in the care with which we celebrate them.

As long as one was only concerned about sacraments as abstract means of grace, one could be relatively indifferent as to how the sacraments were celebrated. It is still not uncommon for clergy to lampoon serious concern about how the sacraments are performed as obsession with trivia. After all, we are supposed to be "spiritual," and spiritual somehow still means to many people the opposite of physical.

That simply is not the biblical faith. The Bible is full of accounts of God's use of actions and physical objects as means of self revelation. Jeremiah wears a yoke or smashes a clay pot. Jesus places a child in the midst of a crowd. Actions become means of God's coming to us. Because Judaism knew that God is transcendent and consequently never confused with objects, the Old Testament can speak with confidence of God's acting with things. Christianity, in turn, built upon this concept of transcendence and thereby is freed from fear of idolatry. It can

26

accept actions and things freely. Christianity does not try to out-spiritualize God by evading the physical order. Rather, it is precisely through actions that Christianity discovers God's expression of love to us.

Hence, modern theologies from the sacraments are deeply anthropological. They look at how humans relate to each other and how God relates to us through the sacraments. The two may be different levels but not entirely different realities. In both cases, it is humans who must perceive the self giving. This gives us insight into the importance of observing the actions of people in the sacraments and inquiring what those actions in turn signify to the participants. On that basis, we speak of theology derived *from* the sacraments rather than a theology imposed upon the sacraments or a theology *about* the sacraments.[17]

Hence, we are deliberately avoiding much of the familiar language of traditional sacramental theology. Even the term "grace" has too often tended to suggest some secret medicine injected into us or some mechanical substance we received when we had put the proper coins in the machine. It has been too easy to examine grace detached from the living reality and experience of people, as if grace were an abstract substance, found only in the theological laboratory but not existing in a natural state elsewhere. Our preference is the more dynamic term, "self giving," which is intended to express God's activity in relating to us in personal ways.

Thus, when we speak of sacraments, we are speaking of actions through which God relates to us here and now in establishing or renewing personal relationships. God once acted definitively in the underlying sacrament, Christ, who came into the world to make the Father known. That was not an impersonal entity to be analyzed as to how it causes and confers grace to proper recipients who come to him with the right disposition. Similarly, in the sacraments, we are also dealing with flesh-and-blood realities of how human beings express and perceive life.

God does no less. A useful image of God's action is that of the friend who does not just shout to me from across the street (leaving me to wonder if the greeting was really meant for me or for another) but as a friend, crosses the street to shake my hand (leaving no doubt that I am being addressed). Sacraments are actions through which the power of God is conveyed to us. God not only became human once, but continues to meet us on human terms by divine self giving, through words and actions. Our Creator knows that is how humans are.

III

Words and actions are common to all human life. But it is only within the church that they compose those specific sign-acts we call sacraments. We can never look at sacraments without seeing them in the context of the community of faith. A private sacrament would be a contradiction of terms. A private ordination would come close to a farce; a private baptism is little better. *Sacraments by their very nature are communal.* So it is necessary for us to examine some matters pertaining to the social nature of the sacraments because they deal, not just with individuals or God, but with a community.

Whatever goes on in sacraments happens to an assembly of people. The visible and audible means that make up the sacrament communicate to a group composed of a variety of individuals. This demands, not a private language, but shared meaning, a common language of word and action. What is said and done must have shared meaning so that all can participate. The participants celebrate the sacrament within shared conventions of meanings that they hold in common.

Our concern in this book is to observe as closely as we can what those shared meanings indicate about Christian practice and faith. The question we need ask of each sacrament is "What is going on here?" This is a complex question because each sacrament involves a multitude of shared meanings for the participants. Any simple answers would not do justice to the event experienced in a community. The understanding of the event varies for different people present, but they all hold certain portions of that experience as central and vital or else they would soon cease coming. To find out what is going on we have to come to the sacraments ready to observe and listen.

Our method will be to see what the experience of the sacraments has meant, particularly to the first generation that lived with them, the New Testament church. They had no writings about sacraments to give them approved meanings. They simply experienced sacraments and recorded what those experiences meant for them. In the New Testament we have basically offhand allusions to the sacraments as conventions that readers will recognize. "Have you forgotten . . . ?" Paul begins in one context and elsewhere reminds his readers of the "tradition which I handed on to you." The mysteries they celebrate together are not subjects of theological analysis but of casual illustration, often while making a quite different point, such as the unity of the body or the equality of Christians.

But these experiences of the sacraments of the Apostolic Church, tersely mentioned in the book of Acts and the epistles, had a way of becoming definitive for the Church throughout subsequent history. Reformers in every age appeal to the images with which the Apostolic Church expressed its experience of the sacraments. Thus, this first generation's experience is of highest importance for understanding all subsequent generations' experience of the sacrament. Frequently, even the biblical words became part of the rites themselves, thus further reinforcing these images as definitive expressions of what is going on in the sacrament.

It took the Church many centuries before it began systematic exploration of the meaning of the sacraments individually or in general. No urgency was felt, for instance, in defining in systematic fashion what Christians experienced at the eucharist until the ninth century, and then it was debated without acrimony among the monks. Two centuries later, debate flared up when one theologian went too far. But basically, popular piety took from the sacraments what it needed, and shaped the prevailing theology. Not until the time of the scholastic theologians of the twelfth and thirteenth centuries did theological patterns, instead, get imposed upon the sacraments as they were forced into a system.

Today we try a different tack, a theology *from* the experience of the community that celebrates the sacraments rather than a theology *about* the sacraments imposed on them from an abstract system. Our primary data is what is going on within the social dynamics of the community celebrating the sacraments. Thus, practice should inform our theology, though theology can then help us evaluate the adequacy of practice. There is reciprocity between celebration and reflection upon that celebration. In the liturgical circle, practice leads to theological reflection which, in turn, reforms practice.

When we observe the sacraments, actions must receive equal attention to words, even though we are accustomed to treating theology as a verbal affair. Thus the variety of ways of celebrating any sacrament is important. "What do these actions signify?" we must ask ourselves, and not just "What do these words mean?"

We soon discover a variety of degrees of intensity in what is called the "sign value" of certain acts. One way of breaking bread can be a most eloquent act. Another way can be virtually without meaning. Sign value indicates the power a particular form of action has to communicate. It can be very high or almost insignificant.

Unfortunately, most sacramental theology in recent centuries was more concerned about matters of how to achieve a valid and regular sacrament so that God's grace was conferred. Basically validity is a concept of minimalism.[18] Just how little can you do and still have a genuine sacrament? Baptism demands water, but one can get away with using a thimbleful if necessary. Granted that a tubful would have far greater sign value (because of visual, tactile, and audible impact), but a thimbleful is all that is required for validity. On that level—and that was the level of much sacramental theology after Trent—the sign value of any act received scant attention, if any at all. Validity, as we shall see, has its place. Sometimes we do need to know the bare minimum: no water, no baptism.

But something far more important could easily be overlooked: the humanity of the sacraments. The sacraments communicate within a community of flesh and blood. Real people have to be able to perceive what the sacraments signify, not just receive sufficient doses of abstract grace. Hence, the sign value of any celebration of the sacraments is of paramount importance. Any celebration that ignores the humanity of the participants may be valid and regular, but a complete failure in ministering to people.

We have come to recognize an important new category in speaking about sacraments, namely "quality," that is, the quality of celebration. Quality provides a most helpful concept in promoting reform of sacramental practice. In terms of validity and regularity, most celebrations could be equal. But, in terms of adequacy in expressing God's self giving, some celebrations are far more successful than others, that is, of higher quality. Validity can be determined in impersonal terms of proper form, matter, and ministrant, and yet overlook all the dynamics of a worshiping community. Hence, it was possible for Christians to forget for a thousand years the function of the eucharistic prayer, and not even to insist on a community making thankful remembrance as long as the words of institution were spoken properly.

Once one gets past the obsession with validity—and Protestants certainly are not immune to such concerns—then one can see how vital it is to examine what is signified and how well or how poorly that is done. Quality of celebration becomes a vital concern in seeking adequacy of expression.

The quality of celebration is always related to the social nature of the sacraments. We are not dealing with a private esoteric code, but with something that operates to signify within a community. This is a two-way street. Participation in the sacraments creates community and, at the same time, community that already exists is made stronger by becoming concrete and visible through celebration of the sacraments. The quality of the celebration helps enhance both directions: power for creating community and for signifying that community to itself. Thus sharing in the Lord's supper can create unity. But First Church Corinth was good evidence of how poor quality celebrations could also conceal or destroy unity.

The unity of the Christian community is far more complex than unanimity in belief. The best term for sacraments is still the New Testament term, *mysterion*. Our English cognate "mystery" helps little. When the Bible speaks of a mystery it refers to a way in which God is disclosed to whomever God chooses. It is a self giving that transcends human ability to understand fully, yet can be received in wonder and awe. God's self giving is *mysterion*, beyond our power of intellect. And yet, it is a self disclosure that unites a community through the act of celebrating it.

The Bible repeatedly makes it clear that these holy mysteries belong to a community of chosen people. God's promises are covenants given to a community, not private possessions. Too often, sacraments have been depicted as powers or privileges conveyed to individuals. Many of the problems with baptism stem from undue concentration on what the individual being baptized gets out of it, rather than on what the community does for itself in baptizing an individual into it.

Since the sacraments are social, they require certain conventions, as do all social acts. If we play baseball, it is necessary for everyone to agree that three strikes is all a batter gets and that three outs retires a side. Without these and other rules, no game could be played, for only chaos would result. If we wish to have a pleasant meal together, certain table manners insure common decency, making an enjoyable occasion possible. In one sense, these conventions are restrictions, but in another they are forms of liberation. They enable us to accomplish what we want to do. Chaos would be far more inhibiting. Thus, we usually accede to certain conventions in a social event because we want to be free to do something together that would not be possible without this consent.

We have already suggested the limitations of the term "validity." But, because of the social context, we must still acknowledge the necessity of such a term in its proper perspective. Validity has value as an attestation that certain conditions are attached to God's gifts in the sacraments. One does not baptize in jest; one does not make eucharist without giving thanks; one does not ordain without the

31

consent of the church. There has to be a consensus about what is necessary to perform a sacrament in order for all Christians to recognize it. Validity has not always been conceived in the most significant terms, but there does have to be agreement on the "form," that is, key words stating what is occurring; the "matter," that is, objects used; and the "ministrant," that is, chief celebrant, or celebrants having the proper "intention," that is, will to do what the church does in the particular sacrament involved. Granted, the term "valid" has often been used to excuse a minimalist approach, yet the term has an objective character that complements the more subjective terms "quality," or "sign value." Indeed, validity has a liberating dimension, for once one is secure in knowledge of the bare minimum required, one's imagination is free to try creative innovations that might not otherwise be dared.

At the same time, the concept of "regularity" (or legality or licity), that is, of doing things according to the Church's laws, is necessary if we take seriously the social nature of the Church. Sacraments without the consent of the proper judicatory lead to chaos and division. To avoid dissension, the Church has to decide who can preside at the sacraments and under what circumstances. Laws may be changed from time to time, as the needs of the community change. There are some things it would seem impossible to abrogate, such as the use of bread and wine in the eucharist, or of water in baptism. But the formulas and practices required at confirmation or ordination, for example, can and have changed. Unfortunately, the perversion of regularity occurs in excessive juridicalism or legalism, but these should not blind us to its necessity. At its worst, it is still better than anarchy.

The "efficacy" of the sacraments is a term that has a much more subjective meaning than validity and regularity. Efficacy deals with the possibility of the participants receiving fruits or benefits from the sacrament. This is, not a matter subject to canon law or rubrics, but to personal experience. The efficacy of a sacrament is what validity, regularity, and quality of celebration all exist to promote.

Just how the sacraments are efficacious is a widely debated matter. Most American Protestants tend to take one of two sharply differing approaches. Many are children of the eighteenth-century Enlightenment, affronted by the sense that anything physical can be of spiritual efficacy. So desacralized are they, that they are offended by the very thought that God would use the physical to give Godself to us. Even the term "sacrament" disturbs some, and they prefer the more legalistic term "ordinances." This, in itself, suggests why they continue these observances. Many of them are biblical literalists and cannot evade what they interpret as New Testament commandments: "do this" or, "go . . . baptize." So they feel obliged to continue these practices, but only as pious memory exercises that have some helpful effects on moral behavior.

On the other hand, Roman Catholics and many Protestants consider sacraments to be divinely given means of grace wherein God's self giving occurs here and now. In this sense, they affirm that God does act anew in the sacraments. We do not just remember God's past actions. If God is the chief actor, then the power of the sacraments rests on God alone and is independent of the character of the celebrant. Interpreted in this sense, the term *ex opere operato* simply affirms that the sacraments depend on God alone and are not contingent upon the celebrant. Such a term indicates that sacraments transcend human beings and that we are not dependent upon a gifted leader or limited to our own abilities to conjure up a recalling of God.

Strangely enough, throughout most of its history, the Church has had no clear definition as to how many sacraments there are. Augustine could cite dozens of them. For twelve out of twenty centuries, the actual number of sacraments was indeterminate. And that seems an enviable situation for many today. But the systematizing of knowledge in the twelfth and thirteenth centuries could not tolerate such untidiness. We shall return to the question of the number of sacraments in chapter 4.

Theological speculation about the sacraments finally put an end to such liberty. But it sometimes forgot that sacraments deal, not with systems, but human experience. The Christian community showed long ago that it could live without refined theological speculation about the sacraments; but it would not have survived the first century without the life-giving power of these holy mysteries.

Study of the sacraments must begin in wonder and marvel at what the Church receives in them, and then proceed to reflection in order to understand better that experience. Because the Church is a community, certain doctrines and laws are necessary. Only when these become substitutes for the actual experience of the sacraments themselves do we have to be wary of such secondary developments. The task before us here is to examine the Church's experience of its sacraments, to derive our theology from what the worshiping Church says and does, and then to develop reforms for the practice of sacraments in today's Church.

2

The Gift of Baptism

T he Christian sacraments center around two, baptism and the eucharist. With the first, the Christian life begins; with the other, it is sustained throughout life. They are different means of God's self giving, but they are one, not only in their origin in God's expression of love for us, but also in their operation within the community. The eucharist is the culminating act of Christian initiation, begun in baptism. Thus, we can speak of the eucharist as the only part of baptism that is repeated. Just as it marks the final step of the process of initiation, it also provides strength throughout the lifelong journey in faith. And when death closes out this life, we again recall that the Christian who is deceased has already potentially died and risen with Christ through baptism, and the community that remains on earth joins in eucharist, giving thanks for the life that has been lived.

Baptism is one of the chief means through which Christians perceive God's self giving. It is an event received as pure gift; no one ever deserves baptism. In every case, the person being baptized is the passive recipient of what God does through the action of others. In Orthodox churches, the baptismal formula itself is passive: "So-and-so is baptized." It is not something we do for ourselves; the self giving is God's and the administration of it is another's.

The first step in understanding what God does in this event is to recall what actually happens when we baptize. We shall sketch out the fullness of Christian initiation, recognizing that many churches omit portions or separate them in time. The fullness of the words and actions of initiation is observed only by some Christians, but certain parts are common to all of them.

What happens when Christians baptize? Candidates have been instructed, if they are youths or adults, or parents have been counseled, if the candidates are infants or young children. Sometimes the period of instruction and preparation can extend over months or years. Then, on the occasion designated for baptism, a community gathers in Christ's name, and the candidates are presented to it. They, or their parents, are examined for ethical and creedal commitment to the Christian way of life and community. They may shed or change their clothes and are washed, being plunged into water and raised again. They are dressed in new white garments. Hands are laid on their heads, or chrism (oil) may be poured out to anoint them in the name of Christ, the Anointed One, or both. They are welcomed into the community and join the gathered family of God at the Lord's table for the first time. Further instructions may follow subsequently. All of these actions are accompanied by appropriate words. Most of us are accustomed to more minimal rites than this, often to a few minutes seized at the end of the usual Sunday morning service. But the fullness of the rite and ceremonial can teach us much.

We shall begin our attempt to understand these matters by looking first at what the early Church experienced when it baptized. Then we shall examine two problems of particular urgency for the contemporary Church: the discussion of infant baptism vs. believer's baptism, and the question of the unity of the whole process of initiation. Our treatment of confirmation, or its parallels, will be included in the last section of this chapter.

I

No matter how we baptize, baptism is a rich and varied experience in which Christians for twenty centuries have recognized God's use of human words and acts as a form of divine self giving. The chief problem seems to have been the tendency for Christians to become so delighted by just one aspect of that self giving that we have often failed to notice the rich variety and complexity inherent in baptism as a whole. This has made us value the gift of baptism less than we might have if it had been appreciated in its entirety more often. Frequently, major dimensions of God's gift of baptism were overlooked, as if we were given a radio and appreciated the design of the cabinet rather than its tonal qualities.

The best way to achieve a balanced view of the gift of baptism is by examining what it was that the first Christians experienced in this sign-act. It was obviously a gift received with joy; the New Testament contains abundant references to baptism.[1] Few details are given concerning the actual conduct of baptism; not enough, for instance, to tell us whether infants were baptized with their parents or not. But there are more allusions to baptism than there are to the eucharist. Baptism obviously was known and experienced wherever there were Christians.

We know that the New Testament church practiced baptism from the day of Pentecost on (Acts 2:41). Indeed, there are instances of the disciples baptizing (John 4:2) during Jesus' ministry. For two decades the Church had been baptizing new Christians before our first written documents about baptism, such as Paul's epistles and the Acts of the Apostles, were produced. A generation had grown up in a church familiar with baptism. Thus, from the time we get written documents, baptism was already a common practice.

As documents began to appear, especially as Paul started to write his epistles, what we get are not theological explanations of why Christians baptize. Rather, what we find are images and metaphors in which what is experienced in baptism is referred to in passing as something well known. Thus, we get many glimpses of what the Church experienced when it baptized, though no systematic discussions of baptism itself.

One is struck by the natural form that these images take. They are not cast in theological jargon but in experiences from everyday life: birth, washing, putting on clothes, death, and burial. These images are not abstractions but daily events. Their richness and variety are amazing. Our task here is to sort out the chief images the New Testament writers found natural to depict what the church was experiencing when it baptized others into itself.

We can identify five principal images the New Testament uses to express what the earliest Christians had experienced in baptism: [1] union to Jesus Christ and his work, [2] incorporation into Christ's body on earth, [3] the gift of the Holy Spirit itself, [4] the forgiveness of sin, and [5] new birth. Other minor images are found, too, but the five we shall describe seem to be the predominant ones. All other questions about baptism are premature until we discuss, "What was baptism for New Testament Christians?"

The first form of God's self giving that the New Testament witnesses to as experienced in baptism is that of *union to Jesus Christ and his work*. Paul asks in Romans 6: "Have you forgotten that when we were baptized into union with Christ Jesus we were baptized into his death?" and answers, "For, if we have become incorporate with him in a death like his, we shall also be one with him in a resurrection like his" (6:3, 5). It could hardly be stated more strongly, though Galatians 3:27 is briefer: "Baptized into union with him, you have all put on Christ as a garment." Baptism incorporates us into Christ and his work, especially his death and resurrection. Through baptism, God gives union with Christ, something that only God can give. This is no human effort or aspiration, this is something that can only come as a divine gift from beyond us. According to Paul, God bestows this gift through baptism.

Note the context in Romans 6. Paul is discussing sin. Baptism is an illustration in the course of his discussion. He began with baptism as death and burial. Christians have already potentially died through baptism by sharing in Christ's death, but they have the future possibility of resurrection with him (the same idea recurs in Colossians 2:12). Baptism begins with death and burial but ends with resurrection and life. There is a significant act of burial, the going "down into the water" as Acts 8:38 describes it (the new funeral rites of several denominations begin with references to a Christian as one who has already entered death through baptism). Nature is reversed in baptism: one goes from death to life instead of the opposite. The resurrection becomes future possibility through God-given union with Christ. Thus, baptism always carries an eschatological dimension.

Baptism is a paradigm of Christ's work, centering in his death and resurrection. For, not only are we united through baptism to Jesus Christ himself but to all he does. Christ's work is made ours. We become participants in his eternal priesthood as mediator between God and humans. Through baptism Christians are made "a royal priesthood," baptized and anointed with chrism in the name of Christ. In baptism, "we belong to Christ, guaranteed as his and anointed, it is all God's doing; it is God who has set his seal upon us" (II Cor. 1:21-22). Or again, we "became incorporate in Christ and received the seal of the promised Holy Spirit" (Eph. 1:13). Most likely, early Christians received some form of the royal and priestly signs of anointing or sealing, signifying their becoming participants in Christ's priesthood. Baptism is the foundation of the ministry or priesthood of all Christians. This we call the general ministry of all the baptized.

Closely related to the metaphor of union to Jesus Christ is a second main image, that of *incorporation into Christ's body on earth—the Church.* God's gift, experienced in this instance, is that those united to Christ are also placed within the Church through the operation of the Holy Spirit in baptism. "We were all brought into one body by baptism, in the one Spirit" (I Cor. 12:13). Once again, baptism is only an illustration in this passage, but one sure of recognition for Corinthian Christians. Paul is speaking of the unity of the body of Christ in which the Holy Spirit works, giving each

37

Christian different gifts for the benefit of all. Our vertical relationship to Christ is matched by a horizontal union to each other through the common bond of baptism.[2]

By baptism, Christians are identified with the community of those whom God is saving. Salvation is not a private matter but pertains to life within a community where God's gifts are received. Cyprian and Calvin are careful to point out that there is no salvation outside of the church. By no means does this indicate that all those baptized are guaranteed lives of faith and virtue; it only means that without the environment of faith in which baptism places us, salvation, as Christians understand it, is not a realistic possibility.

The community we are initiated into through baptism is a priestly community, a royal priesthood, in which all have gifts to build up one another. It is characterized by "varieties of gifts, but the same Spirit" (I Cor. 12:4). As parts of the same body, all belong together, for the various ministries "are the work of the same God" (I Cor. 12:6). Christians are a community of priests because of baptism; to each is given gifts and responsibilities for the building up of the others. Within this community of priestly people there is a variety of gifts, given as the Spirit desires.

But there is an equality that Paul repeatedly ties to baptism. "There is no such thing as Jew and Greek, slave and freeman, male and female; for you are all one person in Christ Jesus" (Gal. 3:28). We shall discuss this passage in chapter 5; our concern here is to recognize our equality as recipients. God's self giving is given indiscriminately to all those baptized, regardless of human differences. When we are brought to a place where there is water and submit to baptism, human distinctions disappear, and we become "the people of God, who once were not his people" (I Pet. 2:10). As such, Christians are perfectly free and yet perfectly servants to all. Baptism has been well named the sacrament of equality.

A third form of God's self giving experienced in baptism is *the gift of the Holy Spirit itself.* This is a direct pouring out of God's being, the giver literally is the gift. But the giving is perceived in different ways. Scripture makes abundant reference to the unity of the Spirit's self giving and water baptism. All four accounts of Jesus' own baptism include manifestations of the Holy Spirit. The accounts in Acts make it clear how closely united are baptism and the reception of the Spirit. "While the day of Pentecost was running its course," Peter told converts, "Repent and be baptized . . . and you will receive the gift of the Holy Spirit" (Acts 2:1, 38).

Sometimes the Holy Spirit's timing seems a bit off, for it is poured out at Caesarea before Peter even finishes his sermon, "even on Gentiles" (Acts 10:44-48). While in Samaria the Spirit does not manifest itself on the newly baptized until hands are laid on (Acts 8:17), and likewise in Ephesus (Acts 19:6).

Now, though the New Testament writers are happily oblivious to our late medieval tendency almost to hold a stopwatch to time the exact moment of God's activity in the sacraments, there can be no doubt as to the unity of water baptism and the gift of the Holy Spirit.[3] Whether the laying on of hands, the signing with the cross, or the anointing with oil was the precise moment that marks the Spirit's self giving would have been a meaningless question throughout most of Christian history. The prevailing experience was that baptism and its related rites convey the Holy Spirit. In Acts, the evidence is obvious. The giving of the Holy Spirit becomes apparent in those baptized, often with dramatic intensity. Paul wrote a whole chapter about the manifestations of "gifts of the Spirit" (I Cor. 12). He discusses the "varieties of gifts" found in those who were made to "drink" of the Spirit through baptism.[4] John 3:5 unites "being born from water and spirit," as does Titus 3:5.

Of course, God's self giving as Spirit ties in explicitly with the previous image, that of incorporation into the body of Christ. It is quite unthinkable to be baptized into the Church where the Holy Spirit manifests itself and not to share "fellowship in the Holy Spirit." Ephesians speaks of new converts who "became incorporate in Christ and received the seal of the promised Holy Spirit" (1:13). It goes on to say that this is a foretaste of our entering on "our heritage, when God has redeemed what is his own." And again, baptism is eschatological.

In the third century, Hippolytus uses what must have been a recognized formula, "in the Holy Spirit and the holy Church." Using modern terms, we would say that baptism places us in the environment of faith. By entering the Spirit-filled community, we are placed in immediate contact with the Spirit's self-giving presence. It is misleading to try to distinguish between receiving the Spirit and receiving its gifts, just as it is impossible to separate Christ and his works. The experiences Paul witnesses to in I Corinthians 12 are gifts manifesting the Gift, the Spirit itself.

The New Testament reflects this same experience through other metaphors, such as, "enlightened" or "illumined" (Heb. 6:4) or as "being made holy" or "sanctified" (I Cor. 6:11). These ways of describing the Spirit's gifts, too, are experienced only in the context of the Spirit-filled community. Without the Holy Spirit, there is no

Church; baptism is the sign of its being poured out on individual members for the benefit of the total body.

A fourth image occurs in the biblical witness, namely *the forgiveness of sin*. It is the most visual aspect of baptism, which is, after all, an act of washing. First Peter draws the parallel. "Baptism is not the washing away of bodily pollution, but the appeal made to God by a good conscience" (3:21). Acts is even more direct. "Repent and be baptized, every one of you, in the name of Jesus the Messiah for the forgiveness of your sins" (2:38). And Paul was told: "Be baptized at once, with invocation of his name, and wash away your sins" (Acts 22:16). Paul can speak of Christians as those who "have been through the purifying waters" (I Cor. 6:11). Hebrews 10:22 mentions "our guilty hearts sprinkled clean, our bodies washed with pure water." To say the least, New Testament baptism is very wet. Baptism as cleansing became dogma in the Nicene Creed. "One baptism for the forgiveness of sins" (ICET translation).

Here, more than any place, we could be instructed by the act itself, except that for most of us the washing has become so minimal. A few drops of water, applied to the top of one's head, says very little about God's cleansing act of forgiveness. The promise of forgiveness is much more manifest in a Baptist baptism by immersion or, as throughout most of Western Christian history, when children were dipped in the font.[5] The Orthodox churches still wash them thoroughly. Luther tells us: "Baptism is a washing away of sins . . . for this reason I would have those who are to be baptized completely immersed in the water, as the word says and as the mystery indicates."[6] Other ceremonies reflect the act of washing as in Paul's reference to the newly baptized, putting on Christ as a garment (Gal. 3:27). The pre-baptismal anointing of the whole body that soon developed served much the same function as soap today.

What went wrong that both Catholicism and Protestantism gradually lost such a basic sign of God's action? Both became subject to a sacramental reductionism; as we have said, it is easier to talk about something than really do it. Thus, few churches today have fonts that one could bathe a baby in, even by standing it on its head (which is not recommended).

A different problem arose from the medieval fear of babies dying unbaptized, and thus losing all hope of entering the Kingdom of God (John 3:5).[7] The result was the so-called *quamprimum* practice of getting baptism done as soon after birth as possible. Such a concept is as embarrassing to many Roman Catholics today as it is repugnant to Protestants. But it need not conceal from us what the New Testament church experienced, baptism is a means through which the uncleanliness of sin is washed away and we are united to Christ with a clean conscience. The past is put behind us, and we, members of a fallen race, are given hope through God's gift of forgiveness. Baptism signifies that, through God's action, we are forgiven, we are reconciled. "When anyone is united to Christ, he is a new creature: his old life is over; a new life has already begun. From first to last, this has been the work of God. He has reconciled us" (II Cor. 5:17-18).

Closely related to forgiveness is a fifth biblical image, that of *new birth*. Birth is always a gift, not something that we do for ourselves. Through our being united in Christ, God remembers us as new creatures. Our transformation in birth is not our own doing but what another does for us. Nicodemus is told "no one can enter the kingdom of God without being born from water and spirit" (John 3:5). The gift of baptism brings entry into a new life.

Titus 3:5 says Christ "saved us through the water of rebirth." Baptism marks the beginning for us of a new creation. The old Adam has been put off, dead and buried, our sins are forgiven, and we are united to Christ. Our new birth is a fully corporate experience as we are born into a new body, the Church. Only through baptism can we be born into the royal priesthood of the Spirit-filled community.

New birth is also the most explicitly feminine of the biblical images. The new birth that God gives is, of course, always the act of a woman, whatever the gender of the child born. Thus, when God gives us birth, God gives Godself in a way in which human beings are passive, completely dependent upon God's love and nurture. Perhaps this is why we have been so uncomfortable with birth images and tended to suppress them. The font may be the most female sign the Church has; perhaps this is why we often make it so inconspicuous. Still, at various times, baptismal fonts have been designed to resemble pregnant women and, at the Easter vigil, the font has been explicitly treated as a womb from which those born through water enter a new body, the Church.

God's love for us is made visible in baptism, and these five dominant New Testament images provide our best resource for understanding the operation of that love. Certainly other images appear in the New Testament accounts: naming the name of Jesus, sealing, and entering the royal priesthood are some that find occasional mention. But the five we have listed seem to have been the most central witness to the Church's experience of baptism. In these five images, God's self giving is experienced as uniting, incorporating, forgiving, bringing to new birth, and bestowing the Holy Spirit itself. None is in conflict with another. St. Cyril of Jerusalem called the waters of baptism both "your grave and your mother." Each adds to every other.

The New Testament tells us much less about practice. Even the baptismal formula of words said during the act of washing are unclear, though probably baptism in the name of Jesus preceded (Acts 2:38; 8:37; 10:48) that in the name of the Trinity (Matt. 28:19). The images used to describe the experience of baptism came to shape practice itself for future generations. Paul's image of death and burial evolved after the Peace of the Church into baptistries designed after the fashion of mausoleums.[8] Incorporation into the Church was acted out as early as Justin Martyr by leading those newly baptized into the place of the assembly itself. The giving of the Holy Spirit has been made a visual image in the form of a dove on fonts.

The Church has often failed throughout its history to appropriate the full richness of God's self giving in baptism. There is so much to receive in baptism that Christians have always found it difficult to achieve an adequate balance of the sacrament's riches. Yet any attempt at rethinking and reforming baptism in our time must begin with efforts for achieving a balanced appropriation of the images through which the biblical writers express what the early Church was experiencing when it baptized. Only then can we do justice to God's gift of baptism.

This appropriation of the riches of baptism applies to practice just as it does to theological reflection. The concept of God washing us clean from our sin needs to be given its highest sign value in practice so that washing actually occurs. Without the active participation of a congregation, the whole image of incorporation is dissipated. The sealing of the Holy Spirit (Eph. 1:3) needs the sign of anointing or laying on of hands. These are not peripheral matters but important pastoral matters for giving expression to what God does in baptism. What is done will inevitably shape what is believed about baptism.

II

Only after having thought through the earliest Christian experience of baptism can we reflect on particular problems that have arisen since New Testament times. Even today, we still face major difficulties in realizing and communicating the fullness of

God's gift of baptism. The sacraments always push us to a greater depth than we had expected. We never exhaust their power to help us experience God's love. Any attempted solutions to particular problems in baptism that do not try to recover the full breadth of these biblical images is apt to fall far short of adequate representation of God's gift and human needs.

Two particular problems seem to plague the Church of today with regard to baptism: the debate over infant baptism (paedobaptism) vs. believers' baptism only, and the whole question of the relationship of the rites of Christian initiation to each other. In dealing with both, we face immediately the disparity in American Protestantism between those who see sacraments as means of grace through which God acts in the present, and those for whom sacraments are pious memory aids to help us remember God's actions in the past. There can be little doubt by this point which position we favor here. Our understanding of sacraments as present self giving will obviously influence whatever approach we take in resolving problems of faith and practice. And the resolutions we propose will hardly seem satisfactory to those who operate with a quite different understanding of what a sacrament is and for whom it is difficult to accept that baptism effects what it signifies. This is an unavoidable situation, given the variety of theological perspectives in American Protestantism. This problem colors any attempt to discuss sacraments across, or even within, denominational lines.

Controversy over infant baptism has raged since the 1520s, although rarely questioned before that time. We defend infant baptism within certain conditions. Our chief premise is that *baptism is God's enacted promise to be faithful to us, not our promise to God.* As we have seen, the biblical images present baptism as an act in which God is the primary actor. God gives Godself to us in ways that far surpass anything that we could ask or certainly deserve. Furthermore, this giving is always a corporate experience, experienced within and received for the benefit of the community of faith. Baptism, then, is God's free gift, not contingent upon us or our worthiness. By baptism, God makes us Christians; because of our baptism we try each day to become disciples. But all hinges on what God has done for us through the Church.

Like other conditions of our birth over which we have no control, baptism sets up many crucial possibilities for the rest of life. I had absolutely nothing to do with the conditions of my being born a white, male, American. But baptism does give me hope for overcoming the structures of oppression into which I was born. Many people are Christian because God placed them in a Christian family without ever consulting them. Their parents brought them into the Church by bringing them to baptism. Certainly God can and does act for us without our being aware of it. God's action is not contingent upon our knowing about it. The Bible records many instances in which God acts to change a person's life while that person sleeps (cf. Gen. 2:21; 15:12).

Many become Christians in the way described by Horace Bushnell: "The child is to grow up a Christian and never know himself as being otherwise."[9] They do not choose to be a Christian; God does that and begins fulfilling God's promises in the very act of being brought to baptism by Christian parents. Obviously others come to Christianity at different stages in life. God's promise for them is enacted at a later stage. But nothing suggests that those for whom God enacts this promise late in life become better Christians than those whom God baptizes as infants. In either case, baptism is God's act for us, not contingent upon us, but solely God's gracious self giving. For infant or adult, baptism marks a change in our being, but the change is through God's action, not ours.

Classical rites agree that God acts in baptism in various forms of self giving. But a curious petrifaction occurred: even when the vast majority of persons being baptized were infants, the pre-Reformation rites continued to reflect conditions of adult baptism. Vatican II ordered that "the rite for the baptism of infants is to be revised, and it should be adapted to the circumstances that those to be baptized are, in fact, infants,"[10] a mandate fulfilled in the new *Rite for Baptism of Children* of 1969. When we are confronted with the long period in which children were baptized, even though the rite retained the earmarks of an adult rite, especially in presupposing a catechumenate (a manifest impossibility for an eight-day old child), one is forced to question what determines normativeness. Is it the actual practice of baptizing those for whom a catechumenate was impossible, or is it the presumption of such a stage in the rite itself? Liturgy is not immune from such inconsistencies. The Byzantine eucharist still includes the words for dismissal of catechumens though none have departed for centuries; the Anglican-Methodist eucharistic tradition includes a spoken rubric, "Draw near with faith," but no one has moved at this point in centuries.

What constitutes a norm when words and practice are in conflict? Words are often subject to inertia that makes them less than reliable indicators of what is really happening. It would be inconsistent with the ideas of this book to prefer words to actions.

Thus I find it difficult to agree with Aidan Kavanagh that adult initiation is what the "Roman Catholic *norm of baptism* is henceforth to be"[11] or was in the past. If practice informs our theology, the fact that the vast majority of Christians past or present have been baptized as infants cannot be ignored in determining what constitutes a norm.

Discussions of infant baptism are basically concerned with ecclesiological problems. Unfortunately, most discussions of the subject seem to begin and end with questions as to what the individual baptized gets out of baptism. This is a subsidiary concern. It tends to reflect late-medieval-Reformation individualism: If one does not get something out of anything, that thing does not happen. Everything becomes contingent upon me. But baptism is not an individual matter. It is always an act of the Church whether one person is baptized, a family, or a tribe.

Baptism is the Church's primary form of evangelization; it is how the Church is built up. Whenever the Church incorporates a new member into its body, there is a fresh epiphany to the Church of what Christ has done by dying and rising for it. Baptism reminds us of what it means to be a priestly people. The baptismal font ought to be as prominent as the pulpit; both witness to the same reality, the Savior who had a baptism that we might have life.

Whenever the Church baptizes into itself, baptism gives the whole body responsibility to evangelize and nurture the new Christians by entrusting to it their spiritual and material welfare (cf. Acts 2:44-45), a radical step indeed. Thus, all members of the royal priesthood have a general ministry to each other as they work together with an "aim at one thing: to build up the church" (I Cor. 14:27). Through baptism, we become members of one another, and our mutual priesthood is shown forth in every baptism.

One's approach to infant baptism is apt to be very closely tied to one's ecclesiology. If one believes that the Church is a holy sect of saints, the Church as virgin rather than mother, then baptism for believers only makes more sense. Among Mennonites, the practice of believers' baptism only is a natural consequence of their concept of a gathered pure Church. Most Christians have a church-type image of the Church as encompassing Christians, both lukewarm and deeply committed, a congregation both of saints and sinners. They prefer to leave the sorting out of the wheat and tares to God. This is the pattern of most of America's larger churches. They are churches, not sects. That is not to say that they have no standards; many refuse to baptize a child unless the parents are people of faith who, after counseling, give convincing evidence of serious commitment to rear the child in faith.

Baptists safeguard the purity of the Church at a horrible price, the exclusion of their own children. But one can see inevitable tendencies of bodies as large as the Southern Baptists to move into a churchly ecclesiology. It is worth noting that Southern Baptists now publish annual statistics on their baptism of pre-school children—three, four, and five-year-olds. This stretches the concept of believers' baptism, but is a perfectly natural move as a sectarian mentality is replaced by a churchly one. It is just as unnatural to treat one's own children as outsiders to the body of Christ until they are old enough to receive believer's baptism as it is to say one's children are not Americans until they can vote. If one believes that all Christians live within a priestly community, and the New Testament is quite clear on that point, then adults should surely exercise that priesthood to children, and they to adults. It is easy to argue that children have a special priesthood within the body. Jesus used a child as a model for all who want to enter the Kingdom of heaven (Matt. 18:2; Mark 10:15; Luke 18:16-17).

Ironically, peer pressure can be just as much a factor in bringing about baptisms at the "proper" age for those who practice believers' baptism as it can be for paedobaptists. No system is immune from indiscriminate baptism.

It is no surprise that theologians, such as Jürgen Moltmann[12] and Geoffrey Wainwright,[13] writing from post-Christian Europe, rebel against an undisciplined church-type ecclesiology that has led to the practice of baptizing indiscriminately the children of nonbelieving parents. But it seems presumptuous for them to assume that America and parts of the Third World are doomed inevitably to follow European patterns of post-Christian culture. European theologians seem almost impatient with Americans— we do not seem to get on with it and follow suit. There is ample evidence, especially in the South and Midwest, that America is anything but post-Christian. Indeed, the 1980 elections show that America still resonates to rhetoric that sounds Christian. The reasons why indiscriminate baptism no longer works in Europe (or anywhere else) are quite irrelevant to America where there is no surviving tradition of state religion. In America, there is little or no social pressure to have children baptized. Indeed, parents often have to defend their desire to have their children baptized, especially in the South where antipaedobaptists are in the majority.

Unfortunately, we have given little thought to the ecclesiology of the Christian family. Frequently the baptized children of Christian parents grow up never knowing themselves to be anything but Christian. They may not like a theoretical predestination, but many live by a practical one. Their being brought to baptism through the concern of Christian parents is an act of fulfillment of God's will for them. They know the church as insiders. Through baptism God has acted to make them insiders, not onlookers. Becoming what God has made them, Christians, goes on largely in the family. This is why every threat to the family today also endangers the traditional means of shaping new Christians. Such threats undermine the best locale for catechesis Christians have ever known, the family.

Christianity, after all, is more than a theology; it is a way of life, a network of relationships of love. To include children in the Christian family and yet to exclude them from membership in the body of Christ, seems inconsistent. If children cannot be part of God's community being saved, it is dubious whether adults belong there either. Nor would we want to exclude the feeble-minded from baptism simply because they have not developed full cognitive faculties. Baptism goes much deeper than intellectual cognition alone. It is not contingent upon our maturity and cognitive abilities. Rather, it changes our whole life within a context of loving community relationships, expressed both in family and in the Church.

Even for adults, baptism is a gift, not a reward. It marks the beginning of faith and discipline. We require adult converts to move toward faith since without such they would be engaging in hypocrisy if they requested baptism. But they have the remainder of their life to respond to what God gives in baptism as they grow in faith. As with children, much of their faith remains potential at the time of baptism, instead of being fully actualized prior to it.

Baptism, then, is something done entirely for us by God at whatever age it is received. We can accept God's gift of baptism or reject it, but we can never evade it. It is not an optional act we may elect if we feel favorably disposed to God. For God has already acted in our baptism, guaranteeing God's faithfulness to us and placing us within the only community where Christians know salvation—Christ's body on earth.

It should be clear just how directly baptism at all ages reflects the biblical images we have mentioned already. Obviously God's gift of union to Jesus Christ is not a contingent gift, nor is incorporation into the body of Christ. There is no evidence that the early church

47

did not baptize infants. It would have seemed most unnatural in a Jewish atmosphere to treat children as outside of the covenant community to which their parents belonged. We have evidence that nothing is considered unusual about the baptism of children by the late second century.

There is no particular problem with the Holy Spirit being given to people of any age. Children are just as open to its activity as people of other ages. They perceive relationships of love long before they think cognitively. New birth is a miracle at any age, no less or more for the newly born. As they enter the new body, the Church, children receive a new identity, just as when born into a human family.

Doubts have arisen over the need of infants to receive forgiveness. The traditional connection to the forgiveness of the guilt of original sin is less than satisfactory. But baptism is also proclamation of God's will to forgive throughout life and for the recurring needs of reconciliation (see chapter 4). In this sense, baptism, regardless of age, wipes the slate clean so that we start afresh through God's self giving. But it also initiates us into a lifelong process of reconciliation in which we encounter other self-giving acts of God.

The debates over infant baptism continue. The theological debates of Karl Barth and Oscar Cullmann have become almost classic,[14] while the historical debates of Joachim Jeremias and Kurt Aland are likewise important.[15] More recently, Paul Jewett has proposed only "believer baptism" in *Infant Baptism and the Covenant of Grace*,[16] but Geoffrey Bromiley affirms the alternative in *Children of Promise: The Case for Baptizing Infants*.[17] From the Roman Catholic side, Aidan Kavanagh shows a most negative attitude to what he calls at best the "benign abnormality"[18] of infant baptism as contrasted to Eugene Maly's somewhat hesitant defense, "Still a Case for Infant Baptism?"[19] The subject has been accorded an instruction from the Sacred Congregation for the Doctrine of the Faith defending infant baptism, though not the abuses of indiscriminate practice of it.[20]

Certainly all churches need some reforms in baptismal practice. The baptism of children of uninstructed and uncounseled parents (as is common) weakens the case for infant baptism gravely, just as baptizing uncatechized adults (as frequently happens) can bring believers' baptism into question at times. Practices pursued without reflection often become quite dubious.

In short, all those initiated into the body of Christ through baptism are equals because all are passive recipients of God's self giving. At whatever age we come, we are still dependent children, receiving what God freely offers.

III

There is a different type of problem that confronts all Western churches whether they practice infant baptism or not, namely that of fractured initiation rites. Those that baptize infants, usually confirm after an interval of from seven to eighteen years, and give first communion at yet another date. Even those that practice only believers' baptism have rarely seen its relation to the Lord's supper. The Orthodox churches have kept the initiatory process intact, usually at birth. They often encounter other problems, though, such as that all Russians born before 1917 are likely to have been baptized, but baptism has no meaning for modern Soviets. In the West, the process of initiation very slowly got wrenched asunder, requiring sixteen centuries before the Western church finally made the splintering official (the future Queen Elizabeth First was confirmed three days after birth, as late as 1533).

The reformation churches, when they retained confirmation, or something comparable to it, not only canonized the late medieval separation of confirmation from baptism, but also tended to make confirmation a graduation exercise, suggesting the completion of one's religious education. Out of such a disaster has grown a confirmation industry in this country. Ever since the Middle Ages, confirmation has been a practice searching desperately for a theology.

Such a situation seems increasingly unworkable. If baptism means all that it did for the New Testament church, what is the need for confirmation? If catechesis is a lifelong endeavor of learning and applying Christian faith, do we want a putative graduation exercise to interrupt it? Even more important, what does God give at confirmation that is not already given at baptism? Is confirmation purely a non-sacramental human exercise in which we do not expect to experience God's activity? We have problems.

Fortunately, we are also developing some possible solutions. To be as brief as possible, we shall present two theses: *Christian initiation ought to be complete at one time. Christian initiation ought to be a lifelong process.* Those statements seem contradictory, but they are the theses on which Lutherans, Episcopalians, and

United Methodists[21] developed their new initiation rites in the late 1970s along parallel lines.

Both of these statements demand interpretation. The first thesis is that Christian initiation ought to be complete on one occasion. We are not baptized into Christ's death and resurrection for only halfway membership. Nor were we incorporated into the body of Christ with any reservations. Our welcome into the Spirit-filled community is total. Therefore, the ancient practice of completing initiation on one occasion, especially at sunrise on Easter morning, still seems unsurpassed. Anything that suggests that the Holy Spirit is divided between baptism and confirmation ought to be avoided. Thus, the new rites suggest baptism, laying on of hands, and first communion, all on one occasion. The completeness of God's action is made manifest in one rite, witnessing dramatically to all five of the New Testament dimensions of baptism. The sign of God's gift of self is no longer split. Confirmation[22] as a separate rite has been downplayed in the new rites, though it has proved impossible to eliminate the term itself.

But the other thesis is also true; we need to remember throughout our entire lifetime the gift of Godself received in our baptism. Accordingly, the various churches have developed similar rites for affirmation, reaffirmation, or renewal of baptism. Typical is the new United Methodist practice on one occasion each year of sprinkling the congregation and saying, "Remember your baptism and be thankful." That sums it up most succinctly. We never outlive or outgrow the day when we need to recall with thanksgiving God's self giving to us in baptism and to see it continuing daily in our lives. These new services reflect the renewal of baptismal vows at the Easter vigil (introduced in the Roman Holy Week rite in 1955) or the eighteenth-century Methodist tradition of annual covenant renewal services. But they also relate to our modern recognition that human beings continue to become new persons as they develop through the various stages of life. Thus, it is appropriate to renew at annual intervals our thankfulness for what God did once and for all in our baptism. Our baptism is permanent, but renewal of it is a lifelong process.

No doubt we shall see other attempts at resolving the problems of the unity of Christian initiation. But, at the present moment, these new developments seem to be the most promising available when infants are baptized. There is much current excitement in Roman Catholic circles about the new *Rite of Christian Initiation of*

Adults. This refers only to adult converts, and culminates a process of catechesis with baptism, laying on of hands, and eucharist.[23]

We have tried to sketch some of the theological insights derived from the practice of the sacrament of baptism. Baptism is a magnificent gift to be received with wonder and joy. It far surpasses anything we could imagine or devise, for ultimately, it is God's chosen means of self giving to us.

3

The Gift of Eucharist

For the majority of Christians, the eucharist is the most common form of public worship. Every Sunday is world communion day as Christians in two hundred countries join Christians over the course of twenty centuries in celebrating the Lord's supper, eucharist, mass, divine liturgy, breaking of bread, holy communion, or the Lord's memorial. Christians somewhere have gathered weekly, if not daily, since Pentecost, to break bread together with joy in the risen Lord. Today, it is the most universal form of public worship the human race has ever practiced.

Unlike baptism, the eucharist is a repeated experience of God's self giving that Christians observe from baptism until death. It is also the most direct experience we have of God's self giving. We actually receive physical objects, bread and wine, as the means through which God's self giving takes place. The action of giving is one of the central acts around which all eucharistic rites are structured. Thus, the self giving, which occurs by less direct means in the other sacraments, is acted out dramatically in the eucharist. It is not surprising, then, that the eucharist plays such a central role in Christian worship.

What actually happens when Christians celebrate the Lord's supper? The basic structure of the rite is amazingly similar among Christians of most diverse backgrounds; only the ceremonial varies widely. First, the Christian community assembles in Christ's name. Then, after a variety of introductory rites, God's word is read from the Scriptures. Lessons from both testaments usually alternate with psalmody and hymnody. A sermon is preached making contemporary the word heard in the lessons. Prayer is made for the church and world, especially for those in positions of power and those suffering need or distress. The passing of the peace frequently comes at the conclusion of this portion of the service.

The second half of the service begins with the preparation of bread and wine, often accompanied by the offering of money gifts.

Then the presider gives thanks for God's work, commemorates the work of Christ, and invokes the present work of the Holy Spirit. The bread is broken so that it may be shared by all. Next, the whole community assembles around the Lord's table in order to be given the bread and wine over which thanks have been made. Finally, the assembly scatters into the world.

We shall begin our attempt to understand these words and actions by trying to discern what the early Church recorded that it was experiencing when it broke bread together. After that, we shall reflect on two problems confronting most Protestant churches today: the question of frequency of the Lord's supper, and the subject of admission to the Lord's table.

I

The early Church had been celebrating the Lord's supper for two decades before the first books of the New Testament were written. The breaking of bread had gone on for several decades before the most likely dates that the institution narratives in the synoptic Gospels were put into written form. Joachim Jeremias argues that the Gospels vary somewhat in their accounts because they are written out of the worshiping traditions of several Christian communities in different locales.[1] Thus, our link with the Last supper itself is through the worship life of the communities that continued the practice of that meal and within which these traditions were eventually committed to writing. According to Acts, the church in Jerusalem continued "daily attendance at the temple, and, breaking bread in private houses, shared their meals with unaffected joy" (2:46). We also have considerable knowledge of meals in Jewish homes and of synagogue worship in the first century A.D.

We have in the Gospels, Acts, and epistles glimpses of the experiences of the Christian eucharist from a variety of localities spread around the eastern Mediterranean. Never does the New Testament give us a treatise on the meaning of the Lord's supper, but it does allow us to look over the shoulders of those who were experiencing it daily or weekly and to learn what we can from their experiences. Even their casual comments give insight into what these celebrations meant for them, expressed in images they apparently found adequate for expressing what they were experiencing.

The most satisfactory way of delineating these images still seems to be that developed by the Lutheran archbishop of Uppsala, Yngve

Brilioth, in one of the classics of modern liturgical scholarship, his *Eucharistic Faith and Practice; Evangelical and Catholic* (Swedish, 1926; English, 1930).[2] Brilioth treats in historical fashion five key images from the New Testament: joyful thanksgiving, commemoration, communion or fellowship, sacrifice, and Christ's presence. He traces these from the first century through the seventeenth. We shall add two other images that seem to be of major importance, although not mentioned by Brilioth, the action of the Holy Spirit and the foretaste of the final consummation of things.

All seven images have advanced to prominence or receded from it at various times over the course of history. Not one is contradictory; each supports the others. The strongest eucharistic faith and practice achieve a balance among all seven. But so rich is the outpouring of God's self giving in the eucharist that the Church has rarely found it possible to maintain that balance. Hence, much of the turmoil of the Reformation was an attempt to achieve a better reflection of the New Testament richness and variety in experiencing the eucharist. But even those efforts today seem insufficient as modern biblical scholarship has discovered more about the environment in which the early Church experienced the Lord's supper.

The first image of the Church's experience of God's self giving in the Lord's supper is that of *joyful thanksgiving*. The Greek word, *eucharistia*, in almost every instance in the New Testament means giving thanks to God. Acts notes the tone of the Church in Jerusalem. "And, breaking bread in private houses, [they] shared their meals with unaffected joy, as they praised God and enjoyed the favour of the whole people" (2:46). No mournful dirge this; the eucharist was a joyful feast for the early Church, unlike the penitential rite it all too frequently has been since the late Middle Ages.

Thanksgiving appears as a basic act at the Last supper itself. One thing is clear in the four biblical accounts of this event: the Lord gave thanks. The Church followed his example, most likely utilizing a familiar Jewish pattern with prayer of praise, thanksgiving, and supplication. The emphasis is not on human gratitude but thankful commemoration of God's works and prayer for their continuance.[3]

Thus, there is something very distinctive about the way Christians give thanks. They, too, reflect ancient Jewish ways of thinking and practices. Whenever the Church has forgotten the Jewish roots of its worship, it has tended to lapse into saccharine sentimentality. For salt it usually has substituted sugar, and the flavor has become quite different. Much liturgical reform in recent years has been stimulated by the recovery of these often-forgotten Jewish roots and the realization of how essential they are for Christian worship.

In the first century or early second century, the *Didache* instructs: "Now, about the Eucharist: This is how to give thanks" and begins, "We thank you, our Father, for . . ."[4] In good Jewish fashion, Christians then remembered God's saving acts past and petitioned for those yet to come. Likewise, in the second century, Justin Martyr relates that the president "sends up prayers and thanksgivings to the best of his ability."[5] God's marvelous acts of self giving in the past are recalled and the prayer inexorably moves beyond the present into future reality. "Let your Church be brought together from the ends of the earth into your Kingdom," the *Didache* concludes its prayer.

Intimately related is the second image reflected in the New Testament accounts, that of commemoration or remembrance. The key phrase in Greek is *eis ten emev anamnesin* in I Corinthians 11:24, which may be translated "as a memorial of me." The same phrase appears in Luke 22:19. Few terms are so exasperatingly difficult to translate. The Presbyterian *Worshipbook* makes it "remembering me." Episcopalians and Lutherans use "for the remembrance of me," while United Methodists now use "experience anew the presence." Sometimes it might seem easier just to leave *anamnesis* in Greek and educate congregations as to its meaning instead!

When we "do this," we are making present Christ and his work with all his power to save. It is not a matter of "recalling" or "remembering" someone once here but now gone; hence both those verbs are inadequate. It is a matter of knowing the living presence of the Savior himself as if we were witnesses to his presence in historical visibility. Christ is again present to give himself to us through our re-experiencing his past works. Past events are made contemporary; we have overcome time. We engage in a time mystery where past events become present with all their power to save. Thus, the dynamic of the original event—Christ giving himself for us—exists once again whenever we make eucharist.

In recent years, our understanding of the scope of the events commemorated has expanded greatly. It is not just the passion and death, the resurrection and ascension, that the Church commem-orates in the eucharist, though that is certainly a key part of it. The whole sweep of Christ's work from creation to the Second Coming is recalled in the eucharist. Until recently, the West saw the eucharist as commemorating little more than the events of Holy Week and Easter. The Eastern churches have preserved a commemoration of the totality of Christ's saving works, beginning with creation. It is tempting to speculate how different Western culture might have been in its relation to the natural world had it continued to recall God's work in creation as well as redemption.[6] In striking contrast to previous eucharistic prayers, the new ones—Roman Catholic and Protestant—stress the importance of God's works under the old covenant as well as the new. Creation and redemption lead to anticipation of God's "promised Kingdom." As Paul tells us, each Lord's supper proclaims "the death of the Lord, until he comes" (I Cor. 11:26). Commemoration also includes anticipation of acts once promised and yet to be realized.

Paul is eloquent about a third image, that of _communion or fellowship_ with each other. Our fellowship with each other derives from oneness with Christ. We have seen that one of the ways God's self giving is experienced in baptism is through incorporation into one body, the Church. In the Lord's supper, the breaking of bread is a powerful sign of the unity given by the Church's Lord through this sacrament. "When we break the bread, is it not a means of sharing _(koinonia)_ in the body of Christ? Because there is one loaf, we, many as we are, are one body; for it is one loaf of which we all partake" (I Cor. 10:16-17). The action of breaking the bread itself frequently proves a powerful statement of unity, so much so that many churches simply break the bread in silence.

Once again, one wishes one could leave the term _koinonia_ in Greek. It is a simpler term to explain than _anamnesis_ or _eucharistia_, but no less vital. The unity given here is not just human conviviality; it is a gift given in the breaking of bread, a sharing in the body of Christ. It builds upon the Jewish understanding that a meal binds together participants, a concept Paul points out in the very next verse (I Cor. 10:18). But Paul goes a step further: the unity given through Christ also prohibits union with idols. "You cannot partake of the Lord's table and the table of demons" (I Cor. 10:21). Christ not only includes us within his community, but also excludes allegiance to idols. The eucharistic community excludes compromise with evil.

One of the great rediscoveries of the Reformation was the importance of the eucharist as fellowship. Far from the congregation's being a loose collection of individuals, the eucharist forces the members of the body to celebrate their oneness, a oneness experienced on three levels: "one with Christ, one with each other, and one in service to all the world." This oneness given by union in Christ is also union to each other and responsibility to all God's creation. The fullest sign value of baptism as incorporation occurs when baptism is concluded with the eucharist in which new Christians join in the breaking of bread for the first time. The third-century Church added milk and honey at the eucharist for the newly baptized, signifying for new Christians their entry into the promised land. The eucharist is the only part of baptism that is repeated. Oneness is a gift celebrated each time we celebrate the Lord's supper.

An image that has proved the subject of much controversy is that of the eucharist as *sacrifice (thusia)*. Only recently has the air cleared enough so that we can see the biblical witness itself free from the fog of sixteenth-century controversies.[7] We now recognize how pervasive sacrificial imagery is in the New Testament. The very language of the institution narratives is language of sacrifice: "blood of the covenant, shed for many for the forgiveness of sins" (Matt. 26:28) or, "this cup, poured out for you, is the new covenant sealed by my blood" (Luke 22:20 and I Cor. 11:25). In the context of the Passover festival, one could not have signified sacrifice any more obviously to first-century Jews, for whom the covenant on Mt. Sinai was ratified by the pouring out of blood (Exod. 24:6-8).

Many approaches are possible to the image of sacrifice. The concept of sacrifice within Judaism had a wide range of meanings: communion, expiation, and ratification are some.

Hebrews is particularly rich in sacrificial imagery, in which Christ is compared to both high priest and victim. "He offered himself without blemish to God, a spiritual and eternal sacrifice" (9:14). As the *Didache* shows, the churches quickly applied the prophecy of Malachi 1:11 of "a pure sacrifice" to what it experienced in the eucharist. Hebrews 13:15 also speaks of "the sacrifice of praise," though there is no unambiguous relating of sacrifice and the eucharist in Hebrews.

Recent thought has tended to look at Christ's sacrifice as consisting of his whole incarnation and ministry, not just Calvary.[8] Paul understands Christ's entire ministry on earth as the ultimate self giving, that is, Christ's sacrifice is making "himself nothing, assuming the nature of a slave" (Phil. 2:7). This obedient sacrifice is memorialized in the eucharist. Thus, the eucharist is a memorial of all of Christ's work (sacrifice) on earth. In each celebration, the

Church makes memorial of, and experiences anew, all that Christ has done for us in his sacrifice.

Augustine adapted Hebrews 9:24, "For Christ has entered, not that sanctuary made by men's hands which is only a symbol of the reality, but heaven itself, to appear now before God on our behalf." Through its union with Christ, the priestly community of the baptized offers its worship and thus is united to Christ's own offering of himself "before God on our behalf." The new United Methodist rite speaks of "our sacrifice of praise and thanksgiving, which we offer in union with Christ's offering for us."

Jeremias believes that the sacrifice is a memorial of Christ made by reminding God who is for us, Jesus Christ.[9] We "do this" by remembering before God what Christ has done in giving himself to and for us in history. All we have to offer is Christ, but that is all we could possibly need. In this sense, sacrifice is not our work but Christ's alone, of which we make memorial.

Another possibility, one used by Cranmer, applies Hebrews 13:15 to the eucharist. The Lord's supper is thus seen as the offering of "our sacrifice of praise and thanksgiving." Today, at least, we can go beyond the controversies of the Reformation era and recover some of the rich biblical imagery of sacrifice.

Our fifth image is no less controversial, that of *Christ's presence* in the eucharist. In the institution narratives, Christ identifies the bread and wine with his body and blood. "This is my body. . . . this is my blood" (Matt. 26:26, 28). Paul calls the giving thanks over the cup a "sharing in the blood of Christ" and the breaking of bread a "sharing in the body of Christ." The actions are means of participating in the blood and body of Christ.

Fortunately, in recent times, some of the knots tied in the controversies of the Reformation have begun to unravel. The *Constitution on the Sacred Liturgy*[10] makes it clear that Christ's presence in the eucharist is experienced in several modes in addition to the bread and wine. Christ is also present in the ministers, in the sacramental actions, in the reading of God's word, and in the praying and singing congregation gathered in his name. Acknowledgment of the many levels of his presence as discussed in the *Constitution* and in the papal encyclical, *Mediator Dei*, of 1947 opens many possibilities for ecumenical discussion. Unfortunately, these opportunities were not glimpsed in the sixteenth century either between various Reformers or in controversy with Rome.

How is Christ's self giving experienced as presence? The eucharist is the supreme example of giving of oneself through the giving of a gift. We can put our heart in our hands through giving a gift. Never again will that object be the same because it has been transformed from an ordinary thing into a gift. Afterward, the gift always brings to mind the giver. Power to transform things is unleashed in the act of giving. When a little child picks a dead flower out of the wastebasket to give to a parent it suddenly has a far greater beauty than before it wilted. For it has become a sign of love.

This concept of Christ's presence in the eucharist has acquired the name "transsignification." Christ uses bread and wine in the action of a thanksgiving community to give himself to us. No longer is it accurate to say that the elements are merely bread and wine. They are a gift; the reality of them completely changes because they become means through which we experience anew Jesus Christ. They are his love made visible. To a person without faith, they remain only bread and wine. To those with faith, they become Christ's supreme way of giving himself to us. The gift has become the giver.

We can speak of Christ's presence in the bread and wine as a change in the very being of these elements. They remain outwardly the products of bakery and winery but, to the believer, they have become changed in what is really there, for they have become a gift. And the reality of a gift is far more important than its cash value. Gifts make the giver present to us again, even when he or she may be dead. Their action of self giving absolutely transforms whatever they have given us. So, too, bread and wine are the presence of Christ, for they have become a means through which Christ gives himself.[11]

The scriptures do not speak directly of the eucharist as *action of the Holy Spirit,* yet we need to consider this image, too. It is an almost inevitable one when one reflects on the Spirit's presence in the Church and its action in baptism. Certainly the Spirit is active in the event, the eucharist, which most clearly reveals to the Church its true nature.

In what some scholars regard as "the earliest surviving text of a eucharistic prayer,"[12] Hippolytus records the petition for the Father to send the Holy Spirit on the offering of the Church and to unite those gathered in order that it may strengthen their faith in truth. Apparently this is a Christian development of the Jewish supplication. The Spirit's activity is defined explicitly more than a century later by Cyril of Jerusalem. He tells the newly initiated that in the eucharist, "We call upon the merciful God to send forth His Holy Spirit upon the gifts lying before Him: that He may make the bread the Body of Christ, and the wine the Blood of Christ; for whatsoever the Holy Spirit has touched, is sanctified and changed."[13] Here we have an indication of a central concept in the Eastern churches, the function of the Holy Spirit in the divine liturgy.

Unfortunately, the West neglected this aspect for a thousand years.[14] Calvin makes it central in his theology of the eucharist, but not in his liturgy itself. Wesley makes it important in his eucharistic hymnody, but not in his eucharistic rite. But, now, explicit recognition of the role of the Holy Spirit in the eucharist has become common to all the new liturgies. Light from the East has finally reached us all. At stake is the need to express Christ's self giving as happening here and now within the space and time of the worshiping congregation through the Spirit's activity in immediacy within the Church. The Church is where the Spirit acts, and the eucharist is the center of the Church's life together.

Thus, the whole sign-act of eucharist, from gathering to scattering, is an act of Christ's self giving through the immediacy of the Spirit. No longer do we think in terms of a single moment of consecration, but of the operation of the Spirit making Christ present within the total community and the total rite. Because of the action of the Spirit the Church experiences Christ's sacrificial self giving as, not only past history or future hope, but as present reality here and now in its very midst.

One final image, also not discussed by Brilioth, but certainly biblical, needs our attention: that of the Lord's supper as a *foretaste of the final consummation of things*.[15] The Passover commemorated God's past work, but devout Jews also saw the Passover meal as anticipation of the messianic banquet when all things would be accomplished through the coming of the Messiah. In transforming this event, Jesus built on past and future. He looked forward to eating the Passover again "when it finds its fulfilment in the kingdom of God" (Luke 22:16) and to drinking "it new with you in the kingdom of my Father" (Matt. 26:29; Mark 14:25). For Paul, the eating and drinking "proclaim the death of the Lord, until he comes" (I Cor. 11:26).

Thus, the Lord's supper is an eschatological event, reaching ahead to the limits of time as well as back behind the beginning of time. God's self giving is not complete yet. The eucharist is a foretaste of that which is yet to be. It is no accident that all the new eucharistic prayers refer to the time when "we feast with him in glory" or to "his coming in final victory." We join the Christians of the New Testament in experiencing now the presence of the risen

Lord and yet praying, "Amen. Come, Lord Jesus!" (Rev. 22:20). A key theme in these recent intercessions is prayer for the unity of God's people, much as it was in the *Didache*: "Gather it (the Church) 'together from the four winds' into your Kingdom which you have made ready for it."

Each time the Church gathers to make eucharist and celebrate the sacrament of unity, that day is advanced by anticipation, just as the actions of the prophets advanced the events they foretold. So, in the eucharist, Christians pray and act to bring about that final completion to which the eucharist always points. Then, and only then, will God's self giving be complete. In the meantime, we have a foretaste of that love already made visible in the eucharist.

Seven is a long list, but this catalog of images only shows how rich is the Church's experience of God's self giving in the Lord's supper. It also shows how easy it is to overlook some highly significant portions. How long have wy a penitential approach, so that for many Protestants the eucharist is a funeral meal. In the Netherlands, Protestants wear their funeral clothes and celebrate the Lord's supper on Good Friday. What remains is remembrance and fellowship, important to be sure, but only partial apprehension of God's gifts given in the Lord's supper. And even the remembrance tends to be limited to Calvary. We lost much, but the regaining of the full range of biblical images is an exciting actuality in the Church today.

As we recover the fullness of the biblical images, we see the variety of ways in which Christ, as the underlying sacrament on which all sacraments are based, gives himself to us most directly in this sacrament. We remember his sacrifice and all his other works on our behalf until the end of time, express our thanksgiving, are united to one another, and experience the Holy Spirit as it makes Christ's presence known to us. If it all seems very complicated, it is also beautifully simple, perceptible to the least sophisticated. Here Christ gives himself anew to us just as he once did for all in the Incarnation.

II

Communicating the fullness of these biblical images is the greatest theological and pastoral problem with regard to the eucharist. Only after reflection on what is experienced in the eucharist can we turn to examination of present-day practice. How adequately does our practice reflect the fullness of God's self giving as portrayed in the biblical witness? There are numerous reforms in present-day practice that we shall discuss in chapter 6. But, in this context, we can deal more fully with two major areas of question: frequency of the Lord's supper and admission to it.

For most Protestants, the Lord's supper is an infrequent service celebrated quarterly, monthly, or occasionally. On the other hand, for Disciples of Christ, the Church of Christ, and a large number of Episcopalians, it is a weekly occurrence. There are heritages within the Free Church, Reformed, Methodist, and Lutheran traditions of monthly or weekly celebrations but, in many cases, this fact has been forgotten. Few Methodists, for example, are aware of Wesley's parting advice to American Methodists that the elders "administer the supper of the Lord on every Lord's day."[16] And how many Presbyterians recall Calvin's disgust that the magistrates in Geneva would not allow a weekly celebration? Most Lutheran congregations in this country would probably resist a weekly eucharist despite Luther's practice of such.

Roman Catholicism often seems to have the opposite problem. In practice, the eucharist seems to be the only worship option available, so that it is celebrated daily in many parishes and on all special occasions. Roman Catholic popular piety seems to have painted itself into a corner with no liturgical alternatives to the eucharist. Not a great deal of effort has gone into promoting a daily office of prayer and praise for ordinary people. The result, all too often, has been what one author calls a "trivialization" of the mass in that it has to carry the entire freight of Roman Catholic lay piety.[17] The recovery of the liturgy of the hours in a form adapted for congregational use would allow the eucharist to function as the standard Sunday worship with non-sacramental prayer and praise taking its place on other days.[18]

Nineteenth-century Anglicanism moved from rare (three or four times per year) eucharistic celebrations to a weekly early eucharist in many churches. More recently, the eucharist became the main service. That seems the direction of reform among Protestants in our time. To the question of whether quarterly, monthly, or occasional celebrations are sufficient, the witness of liturgical reformers of our time seems to be a unanimous negative. They propose that weekly celebrations should become the norm as the eucharist is restored as the central service each Lord's Day. There seems to be slow but sure movement in that direction in much of

American Protestantism; quarterly or occasional celebrations move to monthly, and monthly eucharists become weekly.

Yet a number of obstacles still remain to this most basic reform. The obstructions do not seem to be sociological or theological. Sociologically there are no barriers to a weekly eucharist. Disciples of Christ congregations, parallel sociologically those in main-line Protestant denominations and so, increasingly, do Church of Christ congregations, to say nothing of Roman Catholics. Theologically it would be hard to find a case against weekly eucharist, though many arguments may be made in favor of such practice.

One often-heard objection to a weekly eucharist is that frequency would detract from the "meaningfulness" or importance of the occasion. Married couples do not seem deterred by such an argument with regard to frequent lovemaking. The frequency of a meaningful sign does not detract from its power. Probably more significant a deterrent to a weekly eucharist is the penitential cloak that the Lord's supper wears in the minds of many people. They simply do not wish to be reminded of their unworthiness so frequently. They have never learned that fundamentally our sin is irrelevant, that the eucharist is a gift for sinners, that none could conceivably be worthy of it. And there is always fear that the service on communion days will be longer and more tedious. But this is largely a mechanical matter of the method used for the distribution of the bread and wine. This can easily be managed so that such services are no longer than those on non-sacramental occasions.

More often than not, the real objection comes from ordained ministers who fear that a frequent eucharist would detract from their ministry of preaching, a ministry most of them take with great seriousness. Actually, not only is this concern unfounded, but many pastors have found that preaching of the word is greatly enhanced by being in the context of the Lord's supper. William Skudlarek has shown how well preaching and eucharist complement each other.[19] The natural response to hearing God's word proclaimed is praise and thanksgiving, best experienced in eucharist.

All too often, on communion Sundays, ministers have felt pressed for time and settled for a short communion meditation. Of course, if the eucharist were the normal Sunday service, communion meditations would never be needed. Nor is time really a problem if we pay due attention to the mechanics of serving communion. For example, experience has shown that it is possible to do the entire United Methodist rite and give communion to about 150 people within a thirty-five-minute service, which includes a brief sermon.

Preaching is at its best within the context of the eucharist. No longer does the preacher and his or her message have to carry the main weight of the service, making it all too often a personality event. Pastors are not competing with television preachers, nor do media personalities celebrate communion before the cameras. But the sermon, seen as liturgical preaching, fulfills its proper role as an essential part of worship and means of Christ's self giving.[20] Recent reforms in the various churches have tended to move the sermon toward the middle of the service, even when the eucharist is not celebrated. Gradually we are moving beyond the type of service that came to dominate much of the Methodist, Reformed, and Free Church traditions of worship in America in the late-nineteenth century. This type of service placed the sermon and a call to conversion at the end of the service. But, in the worship of presumably already converted people—our normal Sunday congregations—it makes much less sense for the sermon to be the last word. Their worship best responds to God's word heard in lessons and sermon through the corporate expression of thanksgiving in the eucharist.

The current wholesale move among Protestant preachers to lectionary preaching is at heart a return to exegetical preaching instead of topical. It is certainly the most significant improvement in preaching going on today. Now sermons are more likely to be true liturgical preaching by being an integral part of the entire service. Sermons do this best by making contemporary the various events in the whole sweep of the Old and New Testaments. Having the eucharist each week to plunge us into the heart of the Christian mystery leaves preachers free to explore those portions of God's word that have been neglected. They can now preach Moses and Jeremiah and Acts and Revelation, because the eucharist always preaches Christ. One of the two strongest arguments for a weekly eucharist is that it strengthens preaching.

Closely related, of course, is the rediscovery of the reading of scripture as an important act of worship in itself and not just as a springboard for the sermon. One of the immediate consequences of adoption of the ecumenical lectionary is movement to the much richer calendar on which it is based. This has brought about deeper engagement with God's word by confronting us with events in Christ's ministry many preachers used to dodge: his baptism, his transfiguration, his coming Kingdom. More of the fullness of

Christ's historical self giving is being commemorated in our preaching. And the constant recurrence of the eucharist, with its witness to the central events, frees us to celebrate these other aspects of Christ's ministry.

The second of the two strongest arguments for a weekly eucharist is the anthropological one. We have seen in chapter 1 that, being human, we need both words and actions in order to give ourselves to others, and that God does no less. Thus, simply because we are human, we need both word and action. The sign-act of God's self giving in the eucharist is needed because humans express and perceive self giving by seeing and hearing it made manifest.

This has had major impact on the way we celebrate eucharist. It means that a need to search out the full sign value of each of the seven biblical images is necessary. How can we manifest the unity of the gathered fellowship if we do not partake of the one loaf? How can we capture the joyful thanksgiving unless we proclaim an adequate eucharistic prayer? The full scope of remembrance is lost if the reading of scripture and preaching consistently ignore the Old Testament and major portions of the New. An adequate eucharistic prayer is necessary to proclaim the work of the Holy Spirit, or Christ's sacrifice actualized, or the eschatological dimension. The way we celebrate is important.

The one God, who gives Godself to us through word and action, acts in both ways. And the person who perceives divine love in both ways needs a steady, that is, weekly diet of words and action.

III

The subject of admission to the Lord's table is almost as complicated as the question of whom to baptize, but the issues at stake are different and have involved less emotional debate. Still, there are some very important ecclesiological issues that have major impact on pastoral work. There really are three problems: the relation of baptized children to the eucharistic community, the relation of unbaptized people of any age, and the relation of Christians of one allegiance to those of another. We shall discuss them in that order.

Our theology of baptized children and the eucharist cannot afford to ignore the discoveries of the human sciences.[21] In recent years, the developmental sciences have taught us much about how children perceive things. We know that they recognize relationships long before they deal with abstract concepts. Thus, one is forced to ponder whether Christianity is basically a system of doctrines, as adults tend to believe, or whether there is something more fundamental to it, such as relationships of love within a community of people. Any child could tell us, "Church is people."

Psychologists now assure us that children perceive much long before they develop conceptual ways of knowing. A child as early as six months old can know what it is to be included or excluded, especially when food is being distributed. Long before they arrive at levels of analytical reason, children have a profound understanding of relationships of love. The five-year-old granddaughter of a United Methodist bishop, being asked why she went to the Lord's table, replied, "To say hi to Jesus." That comes closer to the truth than many adults could formulate using much more sophisticated language about Christ's presence. To exclude baptized children from the Lord's table on the grounds that they do not fully understand it would, if we followed such an argument out, exclude us all. One does not understand a mystery, one experiences it. And children reared in the community of faith can experience it as well as anyone, perhaps better than some of their adult associates.

The tendency in Western Christianity for many centuries has been to limit the eucharist to adults and to expect the child to have progressed toward conceptual understanding of Christianity before being admitted to the Lord's table. In making confirmation or public profession of faith necessary before receiving communion, the Reformation was only drawing to its logical conclusion a long course of development in the late-medieval West. Historical research has shown how long the practice of infant communion survived in the West.[22] Until the twelfth century, children were given eucharistic wine at their baptism by the priest dipping his finger in the chalice. Unfortunately, growing scrupulousness about the consecrated wine in twelfth-century piety led to the withholding of the chalice from laity of whatever age. Infant communion fell victim to fears of spilling Christ's blood. In the Eastern churches, the practice of communicating the baby at baptism has never stopped; baptism still culminates in eucharist.

The whole question of communion of children is directly related to that of infant baptism. Those who advocate infant baptism rarely realize that they undercut their case when they baptize children and then decline to give them communion until they are "ready" for it. Usually that means when they reach an "age of reason," as if their communicant status were contingent upon being able to profess faith conceptually. As we have already seen, there is a tendency to reunite the rites of initiation so that some churches in the West are recovering the practice of infant baptism, infant confirmation, and infant communion, all at the same occasion.

One can hardly bar baptized children from the Lord's table without questioning their baptism itself. If they have been united to Christ and incorporated into the Church through baptism, one can hardly say that sharing in Christ's death and resurrection do not quite count until they can understand it. What God does in baptism for infants or for adults is not done halfway. It is a lifelong gift that places us completely within the priestly body.

Thus, our humanity and studies in theology and history all suggest that baptized children belong at the Lord's table as much as adults. We have not wished to make baptism contingent upon actual faith in the case of infants; no more do we wish to make the eucharist contingent upon rational ability to explicate faith. Neither sacrament is a reward for faith but a means to its development. The presence of children at the Lord's table reminds adult Christians of how much growth lies ahead of us all. Could it be that this is children's special form of priestly ministry as the whole community gathers around the Lord's table?

The question of admission of unbaptized people of any age raises other issues, both human and theological. Baptism places us within a priestly community and imposes on us responsibility for building up each other. It is not a casual relationship but a deep engagement for each other's spiritual and material welfare. It is wrong for me to let my fellow Christian starve for lack of love or of food. Thus, members of the body operate under a disciplined responsibility to exercise their priesthood in mutual self giving. And baptism defines the borders of that body.

Frequently people worship in our services, occasionally children of members, who have not submitted to baptism. They may be potential members of the Church but not yet actual members. Sometimes it is suggested that it is friendly and evangelistic to invite them to the Lord's table, too. It seems so folksy and friendly to say, "Y'all come."

There are serious reasons to resist this, to limit participation at the Lord's table to those whom God has identified with the Church through the act of baptism. The Church in its heroic days was most firm that only baptized Christians could even be present for the eucharist. Many catechumens met martyrdom before eucharist.

What is intended as a friendly gesture, in fact is a put-down of those whom we hope to attract to the Church. For an adult, conversion is a serious step, not something done lightly or spontaneously with a shrug of the shoulders. The *metanoia* of which the New Testament speaks is a life-shaking event. As the baptismal liturgies make clear, it means transformation of one's ethics as well as one's beliefs. Hippolytus felt three years should be sufficient time of preparation for baptism. The human value of those we hope to attract should not be overlooked. They need disciplining as much as anyone else. In a sense, a request for eucharist is a request for baptism, and counseling could proceed on this basis.

Becoming a Christian, even with the longtime and regular nurture of a Christian family, or after serious study and preparation, is an important event. We do not wish to put the sign before the process any more than to advocate sex before marriage. The sign is too important to be made casual. Much of the current excitement in Roman Catholicism over the new *Rite of Christian Initiation of Adults*[23] is due to the long-term sharing of the whole congregation in a series of rites that witness to and aid in the bringing of a person to Christian faith. It is a process that is spread out over months or even years. The whole congregation joins as a Christian family in leading the one becoming Christian to the moment of baptism. Baptism then leads immediately to the fullest sign of participation in the body, the eucharist. Only then, is one ready to share in the banquet of the priestly community.

To short-circuit the whole process is to say that coming to Christian faith for an adult is a trivial process easily rushed through. Conversion can be the central event of a person's lifetime. One does not get married on the first date, but grows through courtship, counseling, being licensed, until the act of marriage can be celebrated with worshiping Christians. Similarly, learning, disciplining, counseling, and baptism are necessary before celebrating an adult's oneness with the body of Christ through the eucharist.

The participation of baptized Christians in the eucharist of other denominations raises a variety of concerns. For most American Protestants, there are no difficulties in intercommunion of any baptized persons or for clergy of other denominations to celebrate at their altar-table (inter-celebration). Some denominations are more restrictive; some extreme cases only allow those baptized within a local congregation to join in its eucharist. Others restrict communion to members of that denomination, arguing that only those of common doctrinal purity or ethical rectitude should join each other in making eucharist. For some, it is merely a matter of conformity to church law.

Whatever the reasons, this is unhappy testimony to our fallen state. However, the pain of not being able to share in each other's eucharist, or for clergy to celebrate at another's altar-table, may be the best possible incentive to pursue the quest for church unity. We can never forget the evil of church division as long as the sacrament of unity cannot be shared together by all Christians. Thus, our present incompleteness has a visible sign in the eucharist that urges us to work diligently to overcome our divisions so that our Lord's will, "that they may be one" (John 17:11), may be realized.

The eucharist is one of God's greatest gifts to humanity. It is a gift to be received with awe and wonder. Calvin said it well: "And although my mind can think beyond what my tongue can utter, yet even my mind is conquered and overwhelmed by the greatness of the thing. Therefore, nothing remains but to break forth in wonder at this mystery, which plainly neither the mind is able to conceive nor the tongue to express."[24]

4

Apostolic and
Natural Sacraments

God's self giving is experienced in Christian worship at special times in the lives of individuals and their communities besides the occasions of initiation and the eucharist. At various times and places, the term "sacrament" has been applied to mark special events in life's journey or what may be recurring acts of release from guilt or sickness. It is time now to examine some of the most significant of these moments of transition or release.

We have already treated confirmation in chapter 2 as a fragment broken from baptism and sketched current efforts to reintegrate the two. In this chapter, we shall deal with reconciliation (the forgiveness of sin), healing, ordination, Christian marriage, and Christian burial. The common thread on which all these rites are strung is the Church's continued experience that at these special events God acts in self giving for the benefit of individuals and their communities. We shall examine these sign-acts one by one after a discussion of the number of sacraments and the authority on which they depend. Space limitations prevent extensive treatment of each, but we can indicate briefly what happens to people in these rites, the biblical roots, and current directions in practice and faith for the most common of what are sometimes called the lesser sacraments. [1]

I

Throughout most of the history of Christianity, the number of sacraments was not defined. Over the centuries, Christians recognized a variety of ways God's self giving was experienced in worship. Dozens of these forms have been called sacraments at one time or another. Augustine applied the term to an assortment of objects and sign-acts: the giving of salt in baptism, the use of ashes for penitents, recital of creeds and the Lord's Prayer, the baptismal font, and Easter Day. Each of these sacred signs represents something inward and spiritual. For the seven following centuries there was still considerable latitude; as late as 1140, Hugh of St. Victor could consider genuflection, the blessing of palms, the receiving of ashes, and reciting creeds as sacraments. Almost to the end of the twelfth century (1179), the Third Lateran Council could still speak of instituting priests in office or burial of the dead as sacraments.

Such latitude seems strange today, so familiar are we with sharply restricted lists. Protestants recognize two: baptism and eucharist; while Roman Catholics add five more. Our sacramental theology is tidy with all the loose ends gathered up by theological reflection. Yet almost a dozen centuries passed before the Church felt any need to systematize what is experienced in the sacraments. The experience of God's self giving in the sacraments is primary; theological systematization was a rather late secondary concern.

The key figure who pulled together the wide assortment of theological reflections about what the Church experienced in the sacraments (and in many other areas) was a twelfth-century theologian, Peter Lombard, a professor in Paris and (briefly) bishop there. His *Four Books of the Sentences* was completed about 1150 and for half a millennium was the basic theological textbook for western Europe. In order to systematize what the Church had been experiencing in sacraments, Peter found it necessary to list them. "Let us now come to the sacraments of the new covenant; which are baptism, confirmation, the blessing of bread, that is the eucharist, penance, extreme unction, ordination, marriage."[2] By the following century the list had become standard, so that the Council of Trent in the sixteenth century could anathematize anyone claiming "that they are more, or less, than seven."

But one step Peter Lombard did not take—he did not find it necessary to affirm that all seven sacraments were instituted by Jesus Christ himself. Indeed, he tells us that unction of the sick was said to be "instituted by the apostles," though Lombard is clear that Christ instituted baptism and the eucharist. In the thirteenth century, however, theologians added the qualification that all sacraments were instituted by Jesus Christ. That complicated matters enormously. The Protestant reformers, who frequently took medieval concepts to their final conclusion, concentrated upon this qualification of "dominical injunction" and concluded that scripture has clear warrant for only two sacraments explicitly instituted by recorded words of Jesus: baptism and the eucharist. Trent, cagily, declined to specify where in scripture the institution of others occurs, partly because the bishops themselves could not agree. But Trent did insist that the "sacraments of the New Law were . . . all instituted by Jesus Christ, our Lord." Both sides were trapped by late medieval developments: that the number of sacraments could be enumerated precisely, and they all had to be instituted by words'of Christ. And Western Christianity has been riven in twain over this issue for four and a half centuries.

Maybe we can go forward by going backward to times before the twelfth, thirteenth, and sixteenth centuries systematized Christian experience of sacraments. The late-medieval-Reformation effort to catalog the sign-acts in which God works puts theological distinctions ahead of communal experience. The need to defend the catalog by appeal to the highest authority—the words of the Savior himself—reduced the list to legalistic debates over authority. No one denied that God works to forgive, heal, ordain, and so on, but everyone fought over the authority by which these acts were called sacraments.

The problem would be much simpler if we were to admit several levels of authority for sacraments. We suggest that they be looked at as dominical, apostolic, and natural. In relation to Christ's institution of baptism and the eucharist, we seem to have ample evidence, and thus we shall call them *dominical sacraments*. Although we may not have the exact words of Christ at the Last Supper or anything similar about baptism, there seems little room for doubt that his immediate followers practiced both baptism and eucharist with the understanding that this was in obedience to the Lord's own example of submitting to one and celebrating the other. The Church was certainly practicing both from its earliest days in Jerusalem, long before scriptures were written (Acts 2:41 and 46). John indicates baptism by the disciples (but not Jesus) early in Jesus' ministry (John 4:2). And there has been no lapse in the practice ever since. Nor does there seem to be any doubt as to the continuity of the tradition that Paul ties to the Last Supper, which he reports that he had handed on to First Church Corinth. Thus, we have the Church's memories of the words and actions of the Lord himself, plus the Church's continuous practice of obedience to what it believed to be his will and example in instituting baptism and the eucharist. And when the Scriptures were written, we find statements attributed to Christ that reinforce existing practices, apparently common to all local churches (Matt. 28:19; I Cor. 11:24-25; Matt. 26:26-29; Mark 14:22-25; Luke 22:19-20).

But scripture gives us not only Christ's words but records his actions and intentions. We have, for example, abundant examples of Christ's forgiving sin. Certainly there is ample evidence of Jesus' ministry of forgiveness (e.g. Matt. 9:2), or of Jesus' will that his disciples should do likewise (John 20:23). Nor is there any doubt of the apostles fulfilling the Lord's intention (Acts 13:38; 26:18). Paul speaks of Christ's having "enlisted us in this service of reconciliation" (II Cor. 5:18-19). The apostles and their followers carried on Jesus' work of forgiveness as has the Church ever since. Whether we have words of institution is debatable; that we have records of Jesus' actions and those of his disciples is clear. Thus the apostolic practice is evidence of obedience to what the early Church considered to be the will of Christ. And on this basis the practice was retained by the Church.

Closely related is Christ's work of healing; examples abound of his healing work and his sending the disciples to do likewise: "the sick on whom they lay their hands will recover" (Mark 16:18). The apostolic Church obeyed these intentions to heal faithfully. The Acts of the Apostles is full of them (e.g., Acts 3:1-10). James 5:13-16 speaks of what had later apparently become routine healing by elders in local congregations.

The evidence for ordination is equally indirect and equally strong. Jesus obviously chose people to be disciples (Mark 1:16-20) and sent them out on mission (6:7-13), having first empowered them ("he gave them authority over unclean spirits") and instructed them "to take nothing for the journey." John makes it more formal: Jesus greets the disciples and commissions them, "As the Father sent me, so I send you," and transmits the Holy Spirit (John 20:21-22). Apostolic practice did likewise. Suitable people were chosen, there was prayer and the laying on of hands (Acts 6:3-6). There are possible parallels as in I Timothy 5:22, and there are numerous cases of setting apart particular persons for special forms of mission, such as Barnabas and Paul (Acts 13:2-3). As the Lord had done, so did the apostolic Church in choosing representative persons to carry out its mission.

In these three examples—reconciliation, healing, and ordination—we have cases of apostolic practice continuing the intentions and actions of Jesus. Thus, though we cannot call them sacraments of dominical institution, if by that we mean a biblical witness to words and actions of Jesus instituting them as sacraments, we do have the witness of the Church's obedient practice. Thus, we can call them *apostolic sacraments* since their institution can be based on evidence of apostolic practice.

Now, this is not to say that everything that Jesus did initiated a sacrament. The clearest example is the washing of feet (John 13:4-16). It is an enacted parable in which Jesus demonstrates the

73

nature of service and humility and even says, "I have set you an example: you are to do as I have done for you." But it is not a practice the apostles did imitate. The rare mention, as in I Timothy 5:10, is an act of someone in the status of a widow, and is cited as a charitable work along with other similar possibilities, such as hospitality. But it is not a prominent feature of church life even though foot washing reappears in Ambrose's initiatory rites in Milan in the fourth century, among the Church of the Brethren in the eighteenth century, and is part of Roman Catholic and Protestant rites for Maundy Thursday. But the Church's observance and experience in foot washing has been so sporadic one would hesitate to call it a sacrament.

There are other ecclesial acts that have at times been considered sacraments. These include the rites of monastic profession and consecration to a life of virginity. These rites do resemble other sacraments. Monastic profession has clear parallels to baptism and burial, and consecration of virgins resembles matrimony in some ways. But these have neither dominical injunction nor apostolic practice as their origin. Indeed, Paul goes out of his way to say "on the question of celibacy, I have no instructions from the Lord" (I Cor. 7:25). There seems to be no advantage in calling these rites sacraments, even though they have some such characteristics and God's self giving is undeniably experienced in them. But God's self giving is by no means limited to sacraments. They and the word are simply the most important witnesses to such love.

But there is one more type of sacrament. We prefer to speak of the Christian marriage ceremony and Christian burial as *natural sacraments*. Both have been listed as Christian sacraments, Christian burial as late as the Third Lateran Council in 1179, and matrimony made the Tridentine list. Scholastic theologians spoke of matrimony as a sacrament of the old covenant (Old Testament), the one sacrament instituted before the fall of Adam and Eve. The same theologians grudgingly conceded that marriage before the fall was a duty and afterward a remedy against sin. Sacraments under the old covenant included such things as marriage, circumcision, and various purifications and blessings. They were said to typify and anticipate the grace that became a reality through Jesus Christ. But they also point to human experiences of crucial passages or releases common to all peoples. Ephesians 5:32 called marriage a *mysterion* (*sacramentum* in Latin), insuring that it would be called a sacrament in the West.

Biblical references to marriage and funerals are painfully few. The wedding feast at Cana (John 2:1-11) was obviously not a

Christian wedding but, most likely, that of a Jewish couple who were friends of Jesus and his mother. Likewise, we lack details of Christian burial in the New Testament. Certainly that of Ananias and Sapphira (Acts 5:6, 10) would not be typical.

In these cases, we are dealing with life events common to all humanity. In virtually every society there are rites of marriage and observances at time of death. It is no surprise that Christians have adapted the wedding customs and burial practices of Jewish and Roman cultures (and almost every other culture in the world) to their own purposes.

The humanity of the sacraments is reflected in the Church's celebration of normal and necessary human passages that are common to all people as witnesses to God's self giving. Not every human rite of passage has been so treated by Christians. Our secular society provides many more: granting the adolescent independence and mobility through the driver's license, the retirement banquet and gift, the golden wedding anniversary. Christianity historically has been reluctant even to mark puberty. But marriage and death have been treated as moments we can call natural sacraments. In them, the Church sees God's work through the community of faith in supporting people as they enter new relationships to each other and the community.

We shall discuss in turn three apostolic sacraments: healing, reconciliation, ordination; and two natural sacraments: Christian marriage and Christian burial. Whether others belong in these or other categories we do not know, we prefer to leave an open question. There is no more reason to be too precise about God's actions now than there was in the first twelve Christian centuries. We would rather leave the number of sacraments once again indeterminate.

II

The sacrament of reconciliation has long been known as penance or confession, just as other sacraments are often known by a portion of the action (breaking of bread, communion, anointing). The newly popular term, reconciliation, is the best equivalent of the New Testament term *katallassein*. According to Paul, reconciliation is brought about by God alone, "From first to last this has been the work of God" (II Cor. 5:18). God reconciles people to Godself (Rom. 11:15; II Cor. 5:18-19) through Christ and has enlisted us in this service of reconciliation. Christians minister in reconciliation as Christ's ambassadors.

What happens in the sacrament of reconciliation? We are moved by examination of our conscience or some form of introspection to remorse over those ways we have offended God and our neighbor. Sometimes such self-examination comes about through a service of the word in which God's law and grace are presented. Reflection on these leads to realization of the great distance between our present reality and perfection.

Our remorse leads to asking forgiveness of God and neighbor. This may mean a general statement of our alienation from God's righteousness or a detailed listing of specific offenses against love. We may have a general lovelessness to confess or specific acts that have caused hurt to our neighbor. We may confess an attitude of defiance and rebellion to God's laws or some particular ways we have preferred our will to God's.

And then another Christian, acting in God's name, pronounces that we are forgiven. Since Luther, Protestants have generally felt that any Christian could declare to another penitent Christian God's will to pardon. Because of their baptism, all Christians are priests to one another and can declare God's forgiveness. Roman Catholicism generally restricts the right to pronounce absolution to priests. We need another human being or a Christian community to pronounce to us God's gift of absolution so as to know reconciliation to God and to one another.

The end result is renewal of life in which God's act of reconciliation has repaired the breach between us. The sinner comes into a restored relationship with God, similar to that he or she received in baptism, when we knew ourselves to be cleansed from all offenses and to stand guilt-free before God. God, through the Holy Spirit, has moved us to remorse and confession that God might bring us to reconciliation with Godself and with our neighbor. In this sense, reconciliation is a restitution of God's work already accomplished in baptism.

The New Testament church experienced reconciliation and remembered it in a variety of ways. Paul could interpret Jesus' whole work as a ministry of reconciliation. Romans 5:10 paints reconciliation as coming through Christ's death, "when we were God's enemies," and as intensified through his life. Elsewhere, Paul can speak of Christ's work as "the reconciliation of the world" (Rom. 11:15). But it is a work of God wherein human beings pronounce God's self giving so others can experience it. It needs a community of priestly people, "Christ's ambassadors."

Christ sent his disciples out to heal and to cast out devils (Matt. 10:5-16; Luke 10:1-17). After his resurrection, he met the disciples and "breathed on them, saying, 'Receive the Holy Spirit! If you forgive any man's [anyone's] sins, they stand forgiven; if you pronounce them unforgiven, unforgiven they remain'" (John 20:23). In this, Christ gave them authority to continue what he had been doing throughout his ministry. Indeed, much of his offensiveness to lawyers came from Christ's readiness to pronounce the forgiveness of sins, an act that was to them a blasphemous usurpation of God's sole power to forgive (Matt. 9:2-8). This authority Jesus transmits to his followers (John 20:23). And the book of Acts is a chronicle of the exercise of this form of authority as the early Church followed the actions and intentions of the Lord.

It was a ministry not without problems. The Letter to the Hebrews shows the Church wrestling with the question of how to deal with the baptized who had fallen away. "It is impossible to bring them again to repentance" (6:6). It was not easy to decide when and where it might be necessary to limit the Church's ministry of forgiveness. Obviously baptism wiped the slate clean, but if it again became tarnished, what then? The second-century *Shepherd of Hermas* reckoned that after baptism "if a man be tempted by the devil and sin, he has one repentance, but if he sin and repent repeatedly it is unprofitable for such a man, for scarcely shall he live."[3]

By the beginning of the third century, Tertullian tells us of a maturing understanding of the Church's role in reconciliation or penance. Penance was called the second plank (after baptism) for the shipwreck of sin, and was appointed for Christians guilty of flagrant sin. By their sin, they had wounded the body of Christ, endangering all Christians by bringing Christianity into disrepute before pagans. Penance was public and strenuous, but it was better to be embarrassed in public before humans than to be damned in private before God. Christians who had sinned grievously needed to apply the astringent medicine of penance that they might be healed and reconciled to Church and God.

The medicinal analogy has never been surpassed. By penance, God acts to heal wounds that divide us from one another and from God. But it is God who acts to restore us to healthy relationships; our own efforts cannot earn or deserve such health. One may give evidence of one's remorse by certain acts, but the forgiveness experienced is always a gift that God gives. Through it we can experience peace with God and with one another.

Reconciliation always has this dual nature. First, there is a vertical relationship inasmuch as we are reconciled to God from whom we have become estranged through rebellion. We have been disobedient sons and daughters, preferring our own wills to God's. Thus, when we trespass against God's will, we constantly

77

violate our true nature as dependent creatures. Our lives of rebellion against our Creator are like those of the prodigal son who can only experience forgiveness by returning home to plead for mercy. Like the prodigal's father, God welcomes us home "not weighing our merits, but pardoning our offenses."

Reconciliation also heals alienation from our fellow humans, the horizontal dimension. Not only have we broken God's law, but in so doing "we have not loved our neighbors, and we have not heard the cry of the needy." Thus there is a strong social dimension in any act of confession. It is a failure to love others as ourselves, a failure reflected in our treatment of individuals and our relation to humanity in general—that we must confess. In failing to practice benevolence to being in general, we have settled for lesser and more selfish preferences. Even the heathen love those that love them in return. But the radical nature of agape love reaches out in self giving to all God's creatures without hope of return. Often our particular loves are reinforced by our culture and nation. But we have to confess that such particular loves are far less than what God demands of us and can become demonic when such loves put "us" over "them."

God's self giving is experienced in reconciliation from both dimensions of alienation: from God and from neighbor. We are given peace in the knowledge of having been made one with God and the human beings from whom we had been divided. Thus, the experience of reconciliation is that of knowing that our brokenness has been mended, not by our work, but by God's self-giving action. The Pauline sense of reconciliation (brought about by God alone) is reinforced whenever we participate in this sacrament and experience once again wholeness through God's gift.

In several ways, reconciliation is closely related to baptism and healing. We have seen already that forgiveness of sins is clearly identified as one of the forms of self giving that the New Testament church experienced in baptism (Acts 2:38). And, as we shall shortly see, the New Testament also links reconciliation to healing of the physical body (James 5:13-16). Reconciliation is both a renewal of one aspect of baptism and a necessary portion of healing.

In recent years, reconciliation has increasingly become a public service in which Christians together experience at-oneness with God and each other in a rite in which all join. The reformed Roman Catholic rites of reconciliation include three possibilities: private, a combination of public and private, and fully public. These offer some valuable forms of ministry.[4] It is highly dubious that a short act of confession at the beginning of a Sunday worship service has much power to communicate the depth of forgiveness. Occasional services devoted to God's word and reconciliation could do this with much more power.

Much of human sin is corporate in that we as a community or nation are guilty of acts of oppression, and even violence, that none of us would tolerate as individuals. Who is to blame for pollution, the arms race, world hunger? We all have corporate sin to confess as well as individual. Public reconciliation gives the opportunity to reflect upon and to confess both individual and collective sin. And we confess in sure confidence that God acts in giving us reconciliation, the sign of this self giving being the words of pardon spoken in God's name by another human. We who once were prodigals afar off are welcomed home by God's boundless mercy. Both our vertical and horizontal relationships are changed by God's self giving in reconciliation.

III

Intimately related to the healing of the soul that occurs in reconciliation is the healing of the body. God's will is seen to be the restoration of human beings both in body and soul. Thus, it is impossible to separate healing from reconciliation entirely. Ultimately, both deal with the health of the body of Christ. The purpose of God's self giving seems to be wholeness that is experienced spiritually, physically, and socially. This, of course, reflects the nature of creation itself, which, according to Genesis, is created good. "God saw all that he had made, and it was very good" (1:31). Much is besmirched with sin, but the restoration of creation is directed toward its original goodness. Healing is an expression of God's basic gift—life itself. The difference between Creator and creature is our finitude. Thus the sacrament of healing does not always have the fruition that we might desire but that which is best in God's wisdom for us.

What happens in Christian healing? Frequently, God's word is read and may be interpreted. There may be confession and pardon of sin. Then prayer for healing is made. Hands may be laid on or the sick person anointed with oil.

The biblical witness to healing is constant. Jesus seemed to find it impossible to resist the cries for help from the sick or maimed. In this, he was following the examples of many of the prophets such as Elisha (II Kings 4:32-37). The gestures vary: Christ uses mud for healing the man blind from birth (John 9:1-41), proclaims to a paralytic that his sins are forgiven (Matt. 9:2-8), and takes the hand of a girl (Mark 5:41). But the purpose is always the same: the outpouring of compassion as Christ fulfills God's will to health in restoring the goodness of the created order. Probably it was a diversion from his ministry of preaching, but Christ could not avoid the need to match words with actions of love.

It was a power Jesus was anxious to share with his followers. The Twelve were sent out to preach and to heal. Mark reports that "many sick people they anointed with oil and cured" (6:13). After the resurrection, the Eleven are sent into mission with the promise that "the sick on whom they lay their hands will recover" (Mark 16:18). Acts chronicles many such acts of healing; a cripple from birth (3:1-10), "many paralysed and crippled folk" (8:7), an accident victim (20:10-12). Healing accompanied the preaching of the gospel wherever the apostles went. The apostles were following the example and intentions of their Lord, if not his explicit commands.

James 5 is our most detailed discussion of the biblical experience of healing in the post-apostolic age. The elders of the local congregation have two functions at the sick bed. "Pray over him and anoint him with oil in the name of the Lord" (5:14). Prayer is efficacious in both raising the sick one from bed and in forgiving sins committed. Thus, healing of the mind (through confession) and healing of the body (through prayer and anointing) go hand in hand. One cannot heal half a person.

Nor is it a private matter. The elders are directly involved, but verse 16 suggests that other Christians, too, may share in healing. "Confess your sins to one another, and pray for one another, and then you will be healed." Such prayer is "powerful and effective." Healing, like the other sacraments, involves the community.

James indicates one act: "Anoint him with oil in the name of the Lord" (James 5:14). There is a physical act involved, one not uncommon in the ancient world where olive oil was used both internally and externally for medicinal purposes. It is appropriate that some physical act ministers to the healing of the body. Ministering to the sick often produces a frustration in groping for words to express our concern. Often a handclasp, a hand on the forehead, or anointing with oil says what words cannot, especially with a semiconscious person.

In healing we recognize the importance of a tangible act, in this case, touching in God's name. Not only is the laying on of hands a sign of concern by all Christians, but in the biblical witness it is also an expression of a charism for healing by some believers (Mark 16:18). Nor is such an expression of the will to heal confined to

Christianity; Christians simply employ a natural human mode of showing acceptance for the sick by touching them despite their debility.

Of course, Christian healing does not replace other forms of medical attention; the two complement each other. It is difficult, if not impossible, to heal a person distraught in mind and soul. We now know how much of sickness is related to various forms of mental stress. Thus, we experience God's work both through the scientific work of physicians and nurses and through the spiritual ministry of fellow Christians. The two forms are not opposed but rely on each other.

Theological reflection on healing has varied greatly. At its lowest ebb, healing came to be extreme unction, a sacrament of the dying. It accompanied other rites of confession, final communion, blessing, and departure of a Christian soul. Unction came to be the final attempt to gain peace with God in the face of imminent death. Although healing was not disdained, it was not expected. Emphasis was on the finality of the event, and it came to be the farewell sacrament.

Recent years have seen recovery of more biblical and patristic views of the sacrament of healing. It has been seen as a sacrament of hope and faith in which the Church unites to restore one part of its body. Unfortunately, bizarre and spectacular methods of healing still often usurp the attention of many Christians, not to mention the media. And thus Christians have often been prone to write off healing as eccentric to mainstream Christian thought and practice. One does not get that impression from reading the New Testament. So we ought to be able to talk about Christian healing without expecting spectacular cures totally independent of God's work through medical science.

Healing is the response of the entire body of Christ to sickness or injury in some part of the body united by baptism. Thus it is always a corporate expression of faith in God's will to health. And it is a corporate expression, participated in by clergy and laity alike. The forms of ministry may vary from the simple act of being present with the ill person, to prayer, to elaborate ceremonies involving anointing.[5] But baptismal responsibilities include that every Christian persist in prayer for the health of other members of the body of Christ and work for the best medical care of those who need it.

Healing, which may be repeated whenever there is serious danger to health, is an important expression of what it means to inhabit the same body through baptism. It becomes a ministry as significant for laity as for clergy. For both, it is a dramatic expression of hope that God's self giving be manifested in the body of another for whose restoration to health Christians pray. There is no question that the self-giving love of God is also manifested through medical skills. The health of the whole person is reflected in Christian healing in a way that supplements scientific means.

IV

Ordination witnesses to God's gifts to the Christian community for leadership within the Church. In this, it recalls the work of the Holy Spirit in distributing gifts to all the baptized for the upbuilding of the Church. Although only a small percentage of Christians receive the sacrament of ordination, it serves as a sign of the calling of all Christians to service of others. The real focus of ordination is not the individual ordained but the community for whose benefit he or she is ordained. Paul states that "there are many forms of work, but all of them, in all . . . [people] are the work of the same God" (I Cor. 12:6). The gifts necessary for the community differ, but all are given by the same Spirit for the use of different individuals within the Church.

What happens in ordination? First, a person or persons are presented and examined to see if they have been given the gifts and graces the community needs. Candidates may be examined as to way of life (ethics) and form of belief (creed) and as to their persuasion that they are called of God to ordained ministry. The congregation usually proclaims them worthy of ordination and acceptable as its ordained leaders. God's word is read and expounded.

When the candidates have been approved and have heard God's word, hands are laid on them and prayer is made. The form of the prayer, coming from sources as early as the third century, thankfully proclaims God's work through leaders in the past and invokes the present action of the Holy Spirit in pouring out upon those being ordained the same abilities to serve the community well. The laying on of hands signifies the giving of these abilities through God's continual gift of leadership for the Church. The prayer celebrates this gift and petitions for its effective realization in those being ordained.

Frequently those ordained are given instruments, the Bible or a chalice and paten, signifying the basic tools of their trade as ministers of word and sacrament. And then, in the context of the eucharist, some of the newly ordained proceed to share in the ministry of worship leadership.

The New Testament church experienced the need for designated leadership. Jesus had called disciples to learn and work with him in his own ministry. They came at his invitation. When he was to leave them, he promised them the Holy Spirit to continue his presence among them. According to the Fourth Gospel, on Easter "he then breathed on them, saying, 'Receive the Holy Spirit!'" (John 20:21). According to Luke, the Holy Spirit came on the apostles at Pentecost when "they were all filled with the Holy Spirit" (Acts 2:4).

One thing seems clear, the gift of ordained ministry manifested the work of the Spirit in the midst of community. Thus Paul, reflecting on it a generation later, can speak of a variety of "gifts of the Spirit" (I Cor. 14:1) besides love. All the gifts "must aim at one thing: to build up the church" (14:26) no matter how diverse they may be. The analogy of the human body is apt; all parts operate in mutual dependence.

Acts witnesses to the need for a variety of ministries in the setting aside of the first deacons to serve the poor while the Twelve served in the ministry of the word. The "whole body of disciples" shares in choosing those to be ordained deacons. The apostles then "prayed and laid their hands on them" (Acts 6:6). Barnabas and Paul are sent into mission "after further fasting and prayer, they laid their hands on them and let them go" (Acts 13:3). In turn, they appointed elders "in each congregation, and with prayer and fasting committed them to the Lord" (Acts 14:23). Often they must have included a charge to the new elders (Acts 20:28). The Church still recognizes a variety of ordained ministries with different functions.

The laying on of hands seems to be a widely recognized sign for early Christians of "spiritual endowment" (I Tim. 4:14; II Tim. 1:6).[6] It must be used with caution and recalled "to stir into flame the gift of God which is within you through the laying on of my hands" (II Tim. 1:6). Ministry is regarded as a Spirit-filled gift that concretely manifests God's self giving through the work performed by those ordained. Election, prayer, and laying on of hands ratify and enhance the abilities to serve, but these, too, are acknowledged as divine gifts.

For the early Church, ordained ministry had a strong focus in liturgical leadership. This took its most concrete form in the role of the bishop or presbyter (elder, priest). The distinctions between these orders is not nearly as clear in the early period as they later became. But either bishop or presbyter was the person responsible to preside at the eucharist by making the eucharistic prayer. In this role, the presider functioned as a pastoral theologian. Presiders had to be capable of praying what was sound doctrine or right worship (*orthodoxia*, according to Hippolytus), as well as knowing the congregation, in order to express thanksgiving in terms of its life situation. Only the bishop or a presbyter he authorized could perform this function according to Ignatius.[7] It was a function vital for the community's life together and only those competent to make eucharist, that is, to function as pastoral theologians, were ordained presbyters.[8]

Ordination is a communal act, inviting God's self giving in the form of varying gifts and graces necessary for the upbuilding of the community. Ordination is not the conveyance of certain powers for the benefit of isolated individuals. God's self giving, rather, is for community through individuals. A private ordination would be a travesty, rather like a marriage with only the groom involved.

God's gift of talents for ministry is stressed in ordination rites. Most rites include the examination of candidates in order to make public and to ratify this awareness of gifts. Frequently the community has some participation in electing or approving those it ordains. Thus we have ordination in and for a community. The community may be a congregation, a conference, a diocese, or a religious order. But ordination is not absolute for an individual's sake. When the Church ordains, it gives communal recognition to God's gift of leadership by recognizing it in the midst of those whom men and women are called to serve.

Ordination is one of the clearest witnesses to the life of the Holy Spirit in the Church. Like any social organism, the Church needs the leadership of gifted individuals. Ordination recognizes the work of the Spirit in supplying the special gifts needed for ordained ministry and invokes the Spirit to pour out on those being ordained the requisite gifts. Thus, ordination is largely invocation in which the Church acknowledges the source of all power necessary to its life together. In this, it invokes, at the same time it recognizes and give thanks for, gifts that the Spirit already has given for its upbuilding, to all in baptism and to some also in ordination.

We are inclined to distinguish between the providential call by which an individual is endowed with certain abilities and feels persuaded of a call to ordained ministry and the ecclesiastical call in which the Church as institution recognizes that prior call and celebrates it by ordination.[9] God's self giving occurs in both forms of call. Although some great Christian leaders, such as Ambrose and Augustine, were recognized almost on the spot, the usual concern for growth and maturity tends to demand years of theological training and skill development in those whom the Church now ordains.

All Christians are ministers by reason of their baptism. Ordained ministers are no more ministers than other Christians who have entered the general ministry through baptism. But the presence of men and women who are ordained and, usually, supported financially by the Church, is a witness to all the baptized of the nature of their new life within the community of faith. Ordained ministry is sacramental in making visible the ministry all Christians share. The ordination of any Christian minister ought to remind all Christians of their own ministry.

It is somewhat strange that Protestantism, with its emphasis on the holiness of all vocations, has never developed any way of celebrating one's entrance into a secular vocation. Only clergy are accorded such a sacrament, although any vocation that serves a public need is equally sacred, the farmer as much as the preacher.

In ordination, the Church articulates what it means by ordained ministry. For reasons of decency and order, the ordained fulfill some functions that other Christians usually do not (such as ministry of word and sacrament and church order). In the ordination rite, the Church most fully expresses what it understands ordained ministry to be, and in ordaining, the Church clarifies its own experience and thought of ordained ministry.

The new ordinals all stress the pneumatological aspects of ministry. We have moved from imperative statements of authority ("take thou authority") to invocations of the Holy Spirit to pour out gifts for ministry. The Church's utter dependence on the Spirit is thus brought to the forefront.

It is also done in a doxological context. The Church, in ordaining, is also giving thanks and praise to God for the leadership that has been given to shape its life together. Ordination is always a service of thanksgiving and expectation of the continuance of God's work for the Church's behalf. The eucharist provides the most appropriate context for such celebration as we join with all Christians in celebrating a whole history of God's self giving in providing leadership from that of the apostles to that of the newest deacon.

V

Equally joyful is the celebration of Christian marriage. Marriage, of course, is common to all cultures. Our concern is to see in what sense Christian marriage goes beyond other kinds as a manifestation of God's self-giving love. We call it a natural sacrament since it is a part of the order of nature, but it shares also in that of grace. Peter Lombard could say it was the only sacrament instituted before the fall. But many medieval theologians had trouble saying much positive about it except that it was a remedy against lust.

What happens when two Christians marry? They come together in the midst of witnesses for a service that is both Christian worship and a legal transaction. The essence of the rite is the self giving accomplished through words and actions in which man and woman become husband and wife through the exchange of vows and property. Even the vows are the legal terms of conveyance of property, "to have and to hold" and the conditions of such contract. Words become a mode of self giving, reinforced by symbolic actions, such as facing one another and the exchange of gifts (rings or coins in some cultures). The community is present to witness and vouch that there is a mutual exchange freely given. Frequently the giving of selves is preceded by a service of the word and followed by another sign of God's self giving in eucharist.

The biblical witness to the rite of marriage is almost nil. The wedding Jesus attended at Cana (John 2:1-11) was obviously Jewish, and about all we learn is that both Jesus and the steward knew good wine. References to marriage abound in upholding its indissolubility except in case of adultery (Matt. 19:6-9 and I Cor. 7:10-11). Paul gives faint encouragement to marriage as being better than burning (I Cor. 7:9). But, as to the rite by which Christians got married, we know very little. The best we can do is to suppose that the practice of Jewish and Roman cultures was followed, with Christians urged to marry Christians (I Cor. 7:12-16).

Theological reflection cannot escape history, and the predominant history of this rite has been that of the legal contract in the West, a contract which the couple performed and the Church witnessed and blessed. We still speak of the fullest sign-act as consummation—copulation, which could hardly be a public act. So, in effect, the giving of the body was done with words: "with my body I thee worship" as the English prayer book still reads. The Western mentality has been that the couple themselves perform the sacrament and the priest or minister simply assists.

An important alternative is seen in the Eastern orthodox churches. There, the minister of the sacrament is seen as the priest acting for Christ. The event of marriage is an eschatological event as the couple leave the world (the narthex) and enter eternity (the church building) where their union, based on love, is a foretaste of the Kingdom of God where love reigns. Accordingly, the couple are crowned in anticipation of their rule over their future family and as a sign of the Kingdom. An important consequence in the East is that remarriage after divorce is permitted since the priest is the minister of the sacrament, not the couple themselves. One of the problems plaguing the West, the question of the integrity of those who feel compelled to break a lifelong promise, is seen somewhat differently.

Certain legal requirements to civil society are involved in any wedding, Christian or not. Some in our society now raise questions about the necessity of lifelong promises given what we now know about human development. But, it would seem that any contract entered into with less than such an intention could hardly comport with traditional Christian concepts of marriage.

A new dimension has emerged on the basis of Christian teachings on justice, namely, the equality of the partners by virtue of their full human worth and by virtue of their baptism. We shall discuss this in the next chapter.

We cannot avoid wondering why marriage should be regarded as a sacrament rather than simply a legal contract with ecclesiastical blessing. It is not a question easily answered. As Schillebeeckx has shown, most of the history of the Church has shown a real ambiguity by letting civil society follow its own customs for over a thousand years before the Church intervened.[10] And even then it was a slow evolution, finally culminating in the vows being contracted inside the church building only just before the Reformation in England. The Church's reluctance to get involved in weddings, its slow yielding to the need to fill a gap in the development of legal processes, and its late assumption of full responsibility for the rite should be a cautionary signal to us not to impose Christian standards on others.

There has been a trend in recent thought to see Christian marriage as a covenant in which God acts as both witness and guarantor. It is an act performed within a community of faith which, in the newer rites, makes promises to support and uphold the couple. These two reasons assert major differences between Christian marriage and just any wedding held in a church building. Many congregations allow non-Christians to use their building as a service to society. It is a service to society not to be despised and certainly one excuse for occupying such expensive real estate as churches do. But secular weddings are not to be confused with a community using its own (or another's) facility to celebrate the marriage of Christians. The new United Methodist rite is deliberately entitled A *Service of Christian Marriage*, indicating the distinctiveness of Christian marriage.

Christian marriage seen as covenant, witnesses to God's gift of self received through the community, approving, witnessing to, and sustaining the love relationship between two individuals of opposite sex. The act of taking each other through mutual vows occurs in a context of a community witnessing to God's love and promising to be channels God uses to strengthen the marriage covenant. The community witnesses to the act of the couple in joining each other through their vows and adds its blessing to what they undertake.

But even Christian marriage is a curious fusion of pagan and Christian elements. One cannot avoid the cultural mix of Jewish, Roman, and Teutonic, or more recent practices. Placing the *lazo* around the couple in hispanic cultures, the retention of Teutonic practices such as bridesmaids dressed to deceive evil demons (though not eligible bachelors), the Roman fertility rite of throwing rice upon the couple, and many such customs are not remotely Christian. In general, the Church has encouraged the adoption of local customs, partly because it had few actions to offer in their place that were distinctively Christian and more positively, because of knowledge that the practice of marriage is more universal than Christianity itself.

What God does for us in Christian marriage is a self giving of strength and support to human love, reinforced by the presence of the community and the community's blessing. Christian marriage is a matter of covenant with God that a community supports. For Christians, the service of Christian marriage proclaims and creates a new reality of a small church, the family, within the larger church, both founded and maintained by God's self giving as love.

VI

The burial of a Christian is the community's final expression of love for us. It is also the supreme challenge to faith in God for those who have been bereaved. For it forces us to see love even in the mystery of death, the hardest place of all to find it. As late as a council in 1179, the burial of a Christian was referred to as a sacrament and there seems to be sufficient reason to recover this designation. Obviously, burial, cremation, exposure, or some form of disposal comes to all persons, Christian and non-Christian alike. We can call it a natural sacrament in that it has been transformed for those of Christian faith.

This is clear in what happens at Christian burial. Like all funerals, the basic function is disposal of the body in a decent and sanitary fashion. But for Christians this is done in the context of an assembly of fellow Christians in which the strong promises of God in the face of death are heralded through reading from scripture, hymnody, psalmody, and preaching. Then, in the context of prayer, the departed is committed to God's keeping and the body is turned over to the earth, water, or flame.

The biblical witness to the burial of Christians is almost nonexistent. We know that Christians followed Jewish and Roman practices, though transmuted in understanding. The Roman customs celebrating the continuity of the family beyond death, symbolized through ritual meals, made a permanent mark on Christian piety.[11]

The Bible tells us something much more important than burial rites. It proclaims the resurrection faith that Christians assume in their baptism. Since Christ was raised from the dead, Christians can face even death with faith, for they have already potentially died in baptism and live in hope of resurrection. Paul ends his discussion of death in I Corinthians 15 with a song of victory: "Death is swallowed up; victory is won! 'O Death, where is your victory? O Death, where is your sting?'" (vss. 54-55). Paul calls death "a mystery" (51). He writes more a proclamation of God's triumphal love than a theory about death.

For the Christian, burial is an act of God's self giving in which a loved one is entrusted to God's power to resurrect, even in the face of death. The Christian makes no claim to know more about death than another person, but he or she does boast of something more important, a knowledge of God. Thus, though death remains a mystery, it is a mystery within the context of God's love. And that changes the whole picture for the Christian. God's love is the primary focus of Christian burial rather than just our loss.

Other things are at stake, too. The presence of a community of faith in our bereavement is a strong statement of support and love. It does not make up for the loss of a loved one, but it is a witness to an enduring love that surrounds us on earth and the beloved one in God's keeping. God's self giving is experienced socially through the loving concern of others whose very presence in our affliction is a sign of divine love. God's love is made visible, not just in the words and actions (such as committal), but in the assembly itself. Private services miss most of what the Church has to minister to us.

The burial of others also teaches us how to die. Though we are all diminished in the loss of another, we are also instructed in the true nature of our own life. No one is fully mature until that person knows that he or she must needs die, too. Confrontation with death at the funeral of another teaches us the meaning of our finitude and our total dependence on God. It is important for the living to remember the reality of death instead of removing it to the suburbs of our consciousness along with modern cemeteries where the living never venture.

What does Christian burial say to us today? Two things are proclaimed: death is real, but God's self giving in love is even more real. One of the ways Christian burial plays a pastoral function is by not denying the reality of death. Much of the commercial aspect of death in American culture tries to deceive us into avoiding the reality of death by supplying "slumber chambers," "caskets" (never a "coffin") with innerspring mattresses, and "rock of ages" memorials. Medieval people would have been amused by modern superstitions about death. At least theirs were more picturesque!

The reality of death cannot be avoided without causing subsequent damage to the bereaved. Nor can it be ignored without distorting Christian faith. "We shall all die," the woman of Tekoa told David, "we shall be like water that is spilt on the ground and lost" (II Sam. 14:14). Each service of Christian burial makes an important witness to all the living that we are identified with the dead in our own mortality. But it also is the first step in helping the bereaved cope with the reality of separation. Attempts to evade this reality simply procrastinate confrontation with it to a time when the community is not likely to surround them with its loving care. Grief too long delayed can become disastrous. Grief belongs in community that cares.[12]

The second thing that Christian burial witnesses to, unlike non-Christian rites, is that though we know little about death, we know much about God and God's love. We have the example of Christ who has gone before us into death and yet triumphed. As Paul says, "The truth is, Christ was raised to life—the firstfruits of the harvest of the dead" (I Cor. 15:20). Thus we do not face death as if God, too, were helpless here, but as those who discover that God in Christ has already made this passage and risen in triumph.

Every Christian funeral is a proclamation of Christ's victory over the grave. This does not explain death; even Paul is tongue-tied at that point. It is difficult to say whether Christianity even has a doctrine of death. But it certainly has something much more important, a doctrine of God presenting God as the victor, not death. Christian funerals proclaim this victory in the face of death. Anything else would be based on ignorance or evasion. At death, only the love of God counts.

The first purpose of Christian burial is that of consolation of the bereaved in the midst of a supportive community. In the Christian assembly, the reality of death itself is reaffirmed, but an even more important reality is proclaimed, that even in death God's love is victorious.

The second purpose of Christian burial is that of commending the life of the deceased into God's keeping. This includes thanksgiving for the life that has been given. Obviously it is easier to give thanks for a long and fruitful life than for one tragically cut short. Daily, we give thanks for the gift of life itself and for the unmerited favor of the day just lived and for the hope of the morrow. One can never assume he or she deserved to live any day but only in wonder and marvel give thanks for that day. In similar fashion, one cannot avoid giving thanks at the end of a life for the life that the Creator graciously has bestowed upon another. In this sense, the eucharist is a most appropriate way to celebrate the end of a Christian's life. It is the supreme Christian expression of thanksgiving for what has been received as pure gift, life itself.

But even there we are not done; God is not done. For Christians, throughout most of their history, have been willing to pray for the deceased that they may rest at peace in the Lord. We seem safely past most medieval speculations about the geography of purgatory and the dangers of knowing too much. Our knowledge of death itself must remain a reverent agnosticism. But because of the knowledge we do cherish about God, we can pray as we entrust the deceased into the loving care of God. To act as if we could no longer hold them before God after the moment of death is most unnatural. For God's love surely does not cease when our eyes are closed in death. Thus, we can join with our dead through prayer on their behalf. Like them, we too, have borne the mark of death since our baptism and share with them the future of resurrection.

Perhaps the most marked difference between Protestant and Roman Catholic piety is the lack within Protestantism of any sense of the ongoing relation of living and dead through prayer. Historically this is understandable, but Roman Catholicism now has a chastened imagination about what occurs after death. It is time for Protestant piety to venture into a stronger sense of the communion of the saints and the continuity of God's loving care after death as well as before. God's gifts continue as self giving throughout eternity. Prayer for those who have preceded us in death affirms that reality.

Christian burial both consoles the living and commends the deceased to God's continuing care. The community experiences God's self giving through the community's worship that celebrates the resurrection. The community, by its presence, surrounds us with love both in life and in death. God works in witnessing to us of the self giving that has already occurred in crucifixion and resurrection and in their promise of hope for each of us. The Christian burial service remains a sign of this love for those within the Christian community. And thus, though burial is a natural event for all people, for the Christian it is also an important experience of God's self giving.

5

Sacraments and Justice

Traditionally Protestantism has tended to equate preaching with prophetic ministry and the sacraments with priestly functions. An unfortunate distinction has been made between prophetic and priestly aspects of ordained ministry as if they differed in essence. Even more serious is the assumption that the chief aspect of worship concerned with justice is the sermon, while the rest of the sacramental life is not intrinsically involved in such issues. Twentieth-century Protestantism contributed a number of hymns concerned with social justice: "Where Cross the Crowded Ways of Life," "Rise Up, O Men of God," "God Send Us Men," "In Christ There Is No East or West" are examples of hymns that once sounded more inclusive than they ring to contemporary ears. A few leaders, such as Walter Rauschenbusch, wrote collections of prayers such as *Prayers for the Social Awakening*.[1] But generally, many leaders in Christian struggles for justice have seen little connection between sacraments and justice. All too often, a deep concern about worship has been mistaken for a "sacristy-rat" or "cut-of-the-chasuble" mentality, which masks evasion of real social issues.

One can question whether the prophetic and priestly aspects of ministry were ever as distinct in the Old Testament as Protestant scholars tended to make them. But that is not our point here. One could also argue that life itself is not this neatly compartmentalized. But neither does that concern us now. Our concern is that it is shortsighted to overlook the enormous role of sacraments in making both justice and injustice visible in the formation of Christians. Through both shaping and reflecting attitudes and assumptions about the value of persons, the sacraments play a profound role in forming Christians to act in their daily lives. Indeed, the words and acts of a eucharistic service may say more about justice than is proclaimed in the sermon on many occasions. The message of the sacraments, as we have stated repeatedly, goes far deeper than words alone. It is an unfortunate blind spot in many seminaries with glorious traditions of social concern that the sacramental sources of Christian social action rarely get explained to students and are seldom discovered during subsequent careers in ordained ministry. Thus, the false prophetic-priestly dichotomy gets passed on uncritically.

Our concern in this chapter will be to sort out how the sacraments, through their various roles in shaping and reflecting social structures, are intimately involved in issues of justice. We shall examine the relationship of sacraments and justice in general, then analyze baptism as the foundation of justice within the Church, sketch ways in which sacraments can also reinforce injustices within the Church, and then outline the sacraments' mission to justice in the world.

I

First, what do we mean by justice? I shall follow the practice of Professor Joseph L. Allen of defining justice in the context of covenant love as "a recognition of the personhood of each, a refusal to consider any person as of less human worth than any other, and a refusal to reduce anyone to the status of mere means to the good of all the rest. . . . Justice is the expression of covenant love in situations in which rights are involved and a proper balance must be found between competing claims." In this, he utilizes the classical definition from the Roman jurist, Ulpian, of rendering to each one that one's due. This theme has been utilized by Christian theologians such as Thomas Aquinas in his definition of justice as "a habit whereby man renders to each one his due by a constant and perpetual will."[2] But the just course of action is often not easily discerned. What is due to a person in a specific instance may be highly controversial.

The advantage of Professor Allen's adaptation of Kantian terms is that it states Christian justice as exercised in the context of a community living under the commandment to love one another. Thus, a concern for the good of all accompanies the obligation to respect the rights of all equally. In this sense, justice is also an expression of love. Justice is much more than the mere dispassionate meting out of abstract rights to others.

Christians are involved in ways of expressing love as they try to act justly. In this context, the sacraments are intimately connected to justice since sacraments provide means of acting out relationships by enfleshing them in visible forms. There is an ambiguity here because, as we shall see, sacraments can also be perverted to make visible unjust relationships as well as just ones. By their very humanity, they are susceptible to being used in inhumane ways.

Sacraments can become means of reinforcing relationships based on inequality, subordination, and subservience. This can be seen in some wedding services where the bride is treated as an inferior being who comes, not as an equal, but to be subservient to her husband. One could argue that the rite is simply reflecting social reality in many instances. But it goes deeper than that. In acting out those century-old stereotypes of woman's role, the form of the rite can be a powerful force in conserving those concepts, which to many now seem outdated and unjust, as denying woman's full human worth. Thus, frequently the sacraments reflect attitudes that many would hesitate to state overtly. Until Vatican II, the Roman Catholic wedding rite prayed for the woman that she "be faithful and chaste" and "fortify herself against her weakness" without attributing similar failings to the man.

On the other hand, sacraments can be means of enforcing justice as in the fine impartiality of baptism, which is administered to both sexes as equals. So radical is the statement of baptism that, as we shall show, many of the problems of justice within the Church arise out of failure to act out the message and demands of baptism.

Much of the failure to understand these messages lies in the fact that sacraments are primarily actions to which words are joined. It is far easier for habitual actions to go unexamined than words. We might challenge something heard once in a sermon; we rarely analyze something done weekly. *Yet, the impact of these weekly actions and familiar words that accompany them have far greater power to shape us than any single sermon.*

The sacraments often reflect in profound ways unspoken assumptions about the nature of relationships within the community of faith. To understand those relationships, we have to listen to more than just verbal statements about the community; we must observe the dynamics of what goes on as Christians are baptized, fed, married, buried. The actions of the community may betray far more instances of clericalism, sexism, ageism, racism, and ethnicism than we would ever tolerate if such prejudices were articulated. Actions, especially habitual actions, can be so subtle and evasive that they rarely catch our attention. How many of us realized what it implied every time we opened a door for a woman? We did it, not because she might be weaker, but simply because she was a woman. And every time we did it, we reiterated a subtle message of inequality.

Much of the power of the sacraments is that of reiteration. Something habitual often becomes an intrinsic part of us. Repetition reinforces the message so that we accept it unthinkingly. This is both the power and the despair of the sacraments since they can be used to reinforce both just and unjust patterns.

Because of this power, sacraments can be no means of changing attitudes and relationships encountered elsewhere in life. Thus, the experience of equality in baptism may run counter to life on the streets. The experience of the eucharist may raise serious questions about economic justice. Sacraments can oppose culture as much as they can reinforce it. They may be the chief factor giving us a vision of the true nature of the relationship lived daily between husband and wife. And so the funeral may be our only encounter with the reality of death confronted by a Christian perspective.

The sacraments are involved with justice because of their power to underscore the full personhood of a variety of people within a relationship of covenant love. In dealing with the full human worth of these individuals, sacraments can be a profound expression of covenant love, even when competing loyalties may lead to controversy. We shall need to examine how such love is expressed both within the community of faith and in the world outside it. Sacraments deal with both ecclesial justice and social justice.

II

Baptism is the foundation for justice within the Church. It is the sacrament of equality. The earliest record we have of the Church's experience of baptism comes in Paul's epistles. Paul makes explicit in several places the degree to which baptism makes visible equality within the Church. Probably the strongest statement of equality in the whole New Testament occurs in the context of baptism in Galatians 3:27-28. "Baptized into union with him, you have all put on Christ as a garment. There is no such thing as Jew and Greek, slave and freeman, male and female; for you are all one person in Christ Jesus." A somewhat similar passage occurs in I Corinthians 12:13: "For indeed we were all brought into one body by baptism, in the one Spirit, whether we are Jews or Greeks, whether slaves or free men, and that one Holy Spirit was poured out for all of us to drink." A Pauline passage in Colossians 3:11 speaks of the death of the old order and Christians having "put on the new nature" in which "there is no question here of Greek and Jew, circumcised and uncircumcised, barbarian, Scythian, slave and freeman; but Christ is all, and is in all."

There are sufficient parallels in these passages for Hans Dieter Betz to suggest:

> A saying like Gal. 3:26-28 could easily have had its *Sitz im Leben* in the baptismal liturgy. Later Christian liturgies do contain statements similar to the passage from Galatians. One may therefore venture the suggestion that Paul has lifted Gal. 3:26-28, in part or as a whole, from a pre-Pauline liturgical context. In the liturgy, the saying would communicate information to the newly initiated, telling them of their eschatological status before God in anticipation of the Last Judgment and also informing them how this status affects, and in fact changes their social, cultural, and religious self-understanding, as well as their responsibilities in the here-and-now.[3]

It is difficult to agree that we have here a trace of a pre-Pauline baptismal liturgy, much though we would like to believe it. Such liturgical formulae are exasperatingly hard to discover with any certainty, and subsequent use could simply rely on Paul, as often happened. This phrase does not seem to be one that recurs in very early liturgical texts such as the *Didache* or Hippolytus. There are discrepancies even in the wording: differences of sex are mentioned only in the Galatians passage whereas the Jew/Greek and slave/free dichotomies run through all three. Sexual equality is the most radical of all. Greeks could be circumcised, and slaves could be freed, but sexual identity is permanent.

Paul uses baptism as his validation for resisting the human tendency to categorize other humans. The easiest way to deny another his or her full human worth is to place that person in a category. It need not be pejorative. One can easily think of a person as a Texan or a Harvard man rather than a human being as such. When so labeled, people immediately become filed into a slot of preconceived expectations for a person in that particular category. What one expects of Texans or of Harvard men is applied to that person, no matter how totally irrelevant it may be.

Of course, such categorization can become even more unjust when it is tied to derogatory characterizations: blacks do so and so; Hispanics are like such and such. In these instances, we have a kind of stereotyping that is divorced from reality and can lead to very prejudicial judgments. Thus it is easy to generalize, for example, all women like to be treated in such and such a way. But, of course, some do not. Thus the categorization denies the full human worth

97

of those who do not, and even of those who do. The stereotyped image is given precedence over their actual preference, and the worth of their real being is negated.

Paul's comments about baptism emphasize the need to decategorize people in the community of faith. Only by eliminating such distinctions can we grasp the essential oneness in Christ that is given in baptism. Baptism is, for Paul, a means of transcending insignificant human distinctions in order to realize the one important characteristic that does distinguish Christians from all others, their union to Christ through baptism into his body, the Church. Beside that, all other distinctions are indeed irrelevant.

Baptism is also the sacrament of equality because all Christians equally receive it as pure gift. Oscar Cullmann could speak of Christ's *"general* Baptism" in which to "be baptised" for Christ "meant to suffer, to die for his people" (Mark 10:38 and Luke 12:50).[4] He concludes: *"It belongs to the essence of this general Baptism effected by Jesus, that it is offered in entire independence of the decision of faith and understanding of those who benefit from it."*[5] Since Christ accomplished his suffering and dying long before the birth of any of us, baptism obviously is independent of all human abilities to earn or merit it. A fine impartiality is evident since the priority of Christ's action makes our achievements in faith or works irrelevant. The work is Christ's, not ours. Thus, baptism is never a reward for human accomplishment but always a gift from divine love. Nothing we do can merit baptism; we receive it only as unmerited gift.

But it is only as such that it is offered to us, as God's unconditional act to identify us with Christ and Christ's works on our behalf. The love of God operates in ways that are mystery to us.

On this basis, we receive God's act of uniting us to Christ in Christ's work as priest. Through baptism, Christians are made part of "a royal priesthood" (I Pet. 2:9). For Jewish Christians, anointing with oil signified entry into priestly ranks. Paul expresses it: "And if you and we belong to Christ, guaranteed as his and anointed, it is all God's doing; it is God also who has set his seal upon us" (II Cor. 1:21-22). Every baptized Christian bears the mark of priestly ministry through baptism. Aidan Kavanagh says: "The Church baptizes to priesthood; it ordains to episcopacy, presbyterate, and diaconate."[6] All Christians share in the general ministry the Reformation called the priesthood of all believers.

This priesthood is a gift of both rights and responsibilities. Sharing in the work of mediating God's love to others is what it means for Christians to be priests. It reflects Christ's eternal work of being a visible sign of that love of God. Through union with Christ, Christians continue his work in the world by signifying the love of God for the benefit of others. This is both the highest privilege of the baptized and the deepest responsibility. It is inconceivable to be united to Christ, to have put on Christ like a garment, without sharing in his most important activity of being a priestly mediator between God and human beings. Thus, his body on earth is the priestly community, the Church.

All Christians share in this priestly ministry, not because of their own merits, but because of their oneness with Christ through baptism. All receive their priesthood as a gift, not as a reward. What Tertullian said of baptism applies to priesthood as well. "For what is equally received can be equally given."[7] It is as impossible to dissociate priesthood from the gift of baptism as it is to separate Christ from his work. Both are one and the same; both are ours through baptism.

Since baptism is so impartial a gift, Christians receive it equally. As Paul shows, God's gift in it is not contingent on sex, nationality, or condition of servitude. It is indiscriminate love bridging all human distinctions. This applies to sharing in Christ's priesthood as much as to other aspects of God's self giving experienced in baptism. Thus, it seems a refutation of baptism itself to deny the sign of representative (i.e., "ordained") ministry to certain persons purely because of distinctions of sex, nationality, or condition of servitude. The practice of some Protestant denominations, Roman Catholics, and the Orthodox and Oriental churches of denying ordination to women solely on account of their sex seems to be an implicit repudiation of the validity of their baptism. This basic issue of justice within the Church is essentially an issue of sacramental theology. Are women, through baptism, identified with Christ and his priesthood, or are they not? One cannot be baptized halfway. Either one is united to Christ and his work through baptism, or one is not.

Churches that refuse ordination to women, if they were consistent, would also deny them baptism. Anyone who can be baptized into the general ministry ought to be considered a possible candidate for ordained ministry. The New Testament vision sees baptism as making all Christians equally members of the body in which a variety of gifts are used for mutual edification. Until all Christians take seriously what baptism signifies, women will continue to be excluded from ordination in some churches. The scandal of baptism is that it is such a radical breaking down of barriers between people that it is hard for any of us to live up to its fullness.

Baptism is also a repudiation of any form of clericalism that tends to equate the Church only with ordained ministry. All churches with ordained ministers are susceptible to the temptation to treat the ordained as the "real" Christian. Such special functions as the representative ministry serves are indeed necessary to any social organization. But baptism is always the basic gift, given equally to all Christians. Baptism reminds us of our equality as recipients, and puts ordination in its proper context as one means of equals serving equals.

We have already seen that baptism is also a factor uniting people of all ages. All that is Christ's is given to us regardless of our age. The exclusion of baptized infants and children from the Lord's table is questionable since it makes their presence contingent upon cognitive facilities that are not really necessary for experiencing life within a community of love. Thus, baptism is a factor in breaking down the inequalities that differences in age tempt us to use as barriers. Something similar might apply to those who are aged, senile, or mentally immature. Baptism makes such distinctions irrelevant. Baptism is as much a foe of ageism as it is of sexism within the Church.

Obviously the same applies to differences in races. Paul's reference to Jews and Greeks implies that baptism washes away all distinctions based on racial, national, or ethnic distinctions. They simply dissolve in the water of the baptistry. It was common during the civil rights movement of the 1960s to speak of baptism as the sacrament of integration. It is still as relevant today as it was then, though our language may have changed a bit. We might say that the ecclesial rights of all the baptized are equal whatever their race. The Church is a collection of minorities, including the white minority, of the human race. A body is made up of many parts, all essential to the health of the whole. All have equal dignity in its life because all are equally recipients of God's gifts. Beggars cannot boast. All we have as Christians has been given us.

It is important that baptism be a highly visible act in the midst of the gathered congregation. Even when baptism is not being performed, the font or pool reminds us of what we have been given. We have all passed through the same waters and risen in the same body. Baptism is always an eschatological event in proclaiming the nature of true human community in which all racial and ethnic distinctions will have been washed away. We always need baptism to remind us of this. Nowhere else do we see portrayed so vividly racial equality. We are bound to claim as brother or sister in Christ anyone who has gone through the same waters.

Baptism gives us to each other. Differ though we may in outward ways, in the sight of Christ we are one. This oneness we experience as gift that comes from beyond us. Without the self-giving love of God that we experience in baptism, it is impossible to overcome prejudice. Mere human goodwill alone cannot eradicate such evil. Only the self giving we receive from God makes it possible for us to act justly in overcoming prejudice. Baptism breaks down barriers that are next to insurmountable by other means. No caste system can survive its onslaught. Baptism is a constant witness to the necessity of justice within the Church. Every time we share in baptizing a new member into the body of Christ, we hear proclaimed the equality of all persons in the sight of God. Their full human worth is acted out in water.

III

Baptism furnishes the basis for justice within the Church. But it is no secret that the Church frequently is involved in injustices within its own doors. The Church's power for justice is intertwined with an ambiguity; the power for injustice is also present in a community pledged to justice. The sacraments share this ambiguity, too. Since the sacraments are so fully human, they can also be diverted to serve purposes far less beneficial than divine self giving. Just as they can witness to and reinforce the full human worth of all, so unquestionably the sacraments frequently are used to deny that same human worth to many. All of us have been to weddings that make a caricature of justice by reinforcing socially conditioned sex roles. Statements about the husband's obligation "to provide shelter and raiment" and the wife's responsibility "to make a good home for her husband" are still frequent.

One is confronted with the difficulty the Church has in promoting social justice when it often fails to obtain ecclesial justice, that within its own community. How, then, can the Church witness for justice in society if it cannot act justly within itself? Yet, every time the Church denies justice to a majority of its members (e.g., women) or to a minority (e.g., blacks), it vitiates its own power to witness to the world. Much of this denial of justice is carried out, albeit unwittingly, through the sacraments.

An important place to begin is by questioning how the sacraments can malfunction as means of obtaining justice and can become diverted to reinforcing injustice. We must raise questions of the ecclesial worth of individuals as well as their human worth. How completely do we value individuals as members of the body of Christ? Is Paul wrong (I Cor. 12:26) in asserting that all members suffer and rejoice together? When some are submerged by the white male minority in the Church, sacraments may provide the most obvious example of such an injustice.

Sacraments may give us our best clues to uncovering injustices within the body of Christ. And they may give our best opportunity to correct such affronts, not only by teaching us sensitivity, but also by providing an example of just action that is constantly reinforced through repetition. Our sacramental life must undergo constant scrutiny to see if it has been distorted into a means of imposing injustices and oppression. What follows is simply a bare outline of some problems Christians face in discerning whether their own practice uses sacraments as a means to justice or as an evasion of it.

Sacraments include both actions and spoken words. The meaning of actions and the roles of those who perform them can easily be overlooked, especially when familiar. Yet in subtle ways, actions may tell us more about how we value others than the words we use. It is relatively simple to analyze words. If necessary, they can be printed out on paper for all to discuss. But actions often evade such analysis even though they may tell us what we really mean in ways we would not like to hear. The roles we expect people to play often escape discussion because we rarely examine things we have always done. It is best to look at actions and roles before we discuss words.

What does it mean in the wedding service for the bride to be given away? At one time it meant conveyance of possession from father to groom. But what does it suggest today? Certainly not an equality of bride and groom if one has to be led to the other and then conveyed. It may have been part of the past fabric of society, but is it just to act out such subordination today? The whole wedding ceremony remains rife with actions that imply subservience rather than mutual service. Being a star for a day hardly compensates for being submerged for a lifetime. Most of the words have long since changed (Methodists made the vows identical as early as 1864, omitting the bride's vow to obey). But some of the actions still strongly imply a disparity in the human value of the contracting parties or undervalue both. Others suggest the loss of individual being. At a national florists' convention in the late 1960s it was suggested that another item to bill wedding couples for could be two candles, which then are used to light a single one. Somehow, the symbolism was never examined from a theological standpoint. The two may become one flesh, but they still remain distinct individuals, enhanced by the relationship. Neither surrenders selfhood for a merged being (one candle).

Few have recognized the refusal of communion to baptized children as a form of discrimination, but it bears the marks of ageism. Our views on this should be apparent by now. All are as equals within the household of faith, regardless of age.

In some Protestant churches, well-meaning bishops and others who ordain have treated the spouse of the one being ordained as if the spouse were part of the one receiving ordination. The intention is good; ministry is usually shared by husband and wife, whichever is ordained. But the message is bad for it suggests that the spouse is subsumed under the personhood of the one being ordained (who is still usually male) and that the Church gets two for the price of one. The practice is as obnoxious as the phrase "my better half." No one is half of another; we are all full individuals, both ordained and spouse.

There are signs of progress as we become more sensitive to what we do. Until recently, women had to make confession among Roman Catholics with some form of barrier, even a handkerchief, between them and the priest. This was not required for men. Fortunately such discrimination seems to have disappeared. The widespread move to use a pall to cover coffins at funerals is a move to downplay ostentatious consumption even in death. The pall communicates an equality in death, calling attention to Christ rather than to the price of coffins and floral decorations.

Every act of worship is a political statement in the form of roles that people play. Nothing happens by accident, though much may be unconscious. Roles we play in worship often underscore a community's real beliefs about power and authority. Until recently, it was taken for granted that ushers were always middle-aged males looking like bankers who take up money all week and do not enjoy it any more in Church than at the bank. Volunteer organists were usually women, though full-time paid musicians tended to be men. Roman Catholics limit institution into the ministries of reader and acolyte to boys and men, thus communicating something significant to girls. Even the black preaching robe, still widely used among Protestant clergy, is a garment with padded shoulders—equating ministry with physical stature and strength. These are dubious images of a ministry that seeks identification with the weak and oppressed. Clothing, after all, is a means of communication. Increasingly, in Protestant churches, the ancient Roman alb (tunic), a white garment worn by both sexes, and the chasuble, likewise unisex (worn only for the eucharist), seem to be the most appropriate garments for clergy when leading worship.

Much is communicated in the sacraments through the style in which the person presiding actually leads the service. Does he or she preside or dominate? There are distinctive roles for ordained ministers to play in leading the worship of most congregations. But there is considerable variety in the manner various clergy use the powers entrusted to them. A good presider in worship sees his or her role as parallel to that of a presider at the meeting of any group. The person who chairs a meeting well does it with the intention of enabling all members of the organization to participate fully in the business at hand. A bad presider dominates to such an extent that many members do not get to express or defend their opinions. Frustrated silence rather than active participation ensues.

Clericalism, in worship, is that form of injustice where the minister dominates rather than presides. It leads to exclusion from "full, conscious, and active participation" in worship. Lay people could function sometimes better than clergy, in reading lessons, for example. A good presiding (presidential) style seeks to involve as many people as fully as possible, especially a cross section of the worshipers, children as well as men and women. A good clue to presidential style is how frequently the presider sits down, thereby sharing leadership roles with others. If he or she is standing for the entire service, the style is likely to be dominating rather than presiding.

Various actions in the sacraments reflect practices of different races and cultures, especially in wedding and burial rites. Thus, the Hispanic custom of encircling the wedding couple with the *lazo*, or the custom in India of tying a necklace, or the giving of the betel leaf in Sri Lanka are examples of cultural customs. The majority culture tends to negate actions foreign to it. Loud applause may characterize ordinations in black churches but be frowned upon in predominantly white settings. A conscious effort must be made in gatherings that include a variety of races and cultures to include rather than exclude forms of expression that seem natural to minority groups.

Nowhere is this more obvious than in the choice of music. In 1982, The United Methodist Church, for the first time, included Hispanic hymns in Spanish in its English language *Supplement to the Book of Hymns*, though it has long had Spanish-speaking congregations. The hymns and musical styles of other cultures are at last making their way into the hymnbooks and musical life of the dominant culture. Asian-American, Hispanic, black, and native American music is becoming available. It enriches everyone, and it also affirms the human worth of the group that created it. The words of the *Sanctus* are universal, yet the musical setting is usually highly particular, reflecting one culture to the exclusion of all others. But, a variety of musical settings can be used on different Sundays to reflect the variety of humans who sing the praise of God through the *Sanctus*. Music can be used intentionally to be inclusive.

Sacraments also use spoken words. Language is crucial in shaping our apprehensions of reality. The language we use reflects our attitudes toward others. As long as one continues to use derogatory terms for other races or cultures, one is not likely to be concerned about treating them justly. Derogatory labels categorize minorities so it is easier to accord them less than full human dignity. The first step toward treating others justly may be to use different language when speaking of them.

The sacraments are by no means immune to the problems of justice with regard to spoken language. This has been especially true in the case of "sexist language" in which women are subjected to language that is invidious to them or, more frequently, ignores them altogether. Many such problems occur with regard to scriptural materials, though frequently discriminatory language is added gratuitously by translators. Partial solutions are more faithful translations and more attention to the feminine images present in scripture but often ignored. Efforts are underway in both these areas.

Of necessity, sacraments use language speaking of, to, and for God. No easy solution has been found yet to reverse two thousand years of speaking of God as masculine. This is unavoidable in referring to the man, Jesus of Nazareth. Salvation had to take place in a specific and concrete individual, for human beings do not exist without sexual identity. But, when a single gender is applied to God, it is restrictive and arbitrary. No one would want to limit God, but single-gender language does just that in an age that is less and less prone to use pronouns in generic ways. In writing prose today, to speak of God always as "he" is to give a restricted image of God, who transcends all limits, by excluding feminine aspects of the deity. Two possibilities seem to to be available with regard to pronouns when speaking of God: eliminate them altogether by always naming God or mingle them so we speak of her and him alternately. The former may seem a bit impersonal or repetitious at times; the latter is apt to be confusing. Some of us can dispense with most pronouns for God except the reflexive. Here "Godself" seems a necessity. Another development is in employing a wide range of ascriptions of God, especially in addressing God in prayer: "God of all compassion," "God who brings us to birth," "God of justice," and on and on. The search for new (as well as biblical and ancient) language of this type expands one's apprehension of the reality of God. The psalms supply many possibilities.

The language of each sacrament also speaks of, to, and for people. The English language has undergone some major changes in this area in recent years. "Man" no longer is a synonym for humanity. We now realize how unjust and presumptuous it was to use masculine terms as normative for all of humanity. It would, of course, be equally wrong (as well as unthinkable in our culture) to call all people "women." The generic use of terms such as "man," "mankind," and "men" have quietly disappeared from the new Episcopal, Lutheran, and United Methodist services. American Roman Catholic bishops acted recently to remove such language from the eucharistic prayers in use in this country, but the rest of the mass and other rites do not yet reflect this concern.

Especially problematic are many hymns sung during the sacraments. Many of those written to stress inclusiveness during the social movements of the early twentieth century now do just the opposite. One recent hymnal supplement even had to revise "In Christ There Is No East Nor West," changing the word "brothers" to "children." The reference of this hymn on inclusiveness appeared exclusively masculine to present-day eyes when it invited: "Join hands, then, brothers of the faith." The options seem to be either total avoidance of such hymns, or of certain verses in them, or slight changes in the offensive wording. Some hymns we may not wish to sing anymore. Imperialistic missionary hymns, such as "From Greenland's Icy Mountains," are absent from many current hymnals.

There are limitations to changes now possible. At certain times in the sacraments, it is necessary to designate which member of the Trinity one is addressing or to list all three. We do not at present have adequate alternatives for the terms "Father," "Son," and "Holy Spirit." Attempts to substitute functional terms such as "Creator," "Redeemer," or "Sustainer" do violence to painfully developed Christian theology by obscuring the common work of the Trinity. In extreme cases, such usage suggests tritheism rather than trinitarian theology. Yet, the three are distinct as well as one. There are instances, as in the eucharistic prayer, where it is necessary to employ a trinitarian form addressed to the Father, recalling the work past and future of the Son, and invoking the present work of the Holy Spirit. Yet, the Trinity participates in the whole process of salvation. Thus, creation is not the monopoly of the Father, as John 1:2 indicates: "The Word, then, was with God at the beginning, and through him all things came to be; no single thing was created without him."

No alternative term for the first member of the Trinity does justice to Jesus' particular relationship to the Father. Indeed, so radical was the term, when Jews could not breathe God's name, Jewish leaders sought to kill Jesus on grounds of breaking the Sabbath and "calling God his own Father" (John 5:18). Christian worship is often seen as entering into Jesus' own worship of the Father. This is one basis for the Christian use of many psalms. One can more readily enter into this approach to worship if one employs the language of address that Jesus used, namely his constant practice of referring to God as Father. Thus, at various places, such as portions of the eucharistic prayer, the baptismal formula, the Lord's Prayer, and the two ecumenical creeds, we seem, at present, to have no satisfactory alternatives to Father-Son-Holy Spirit language.

We have much learning yet to do. New words such as "Godself" become natural after a year's use, just as addressing God as "you" did a decade ago. Our language must do justice to both the feminine and masculine in humanity and our understanding of these attributes in the deity. It is a process of discovery that will take many years of work and experimentation.

Language is essential in according the full human worth to women and men and likewise to various minorities. In our culture, such terms as "black," "old," "blind," "deaf," "sinister," "aged," "unseeing," "mute," "midget," "dwarf," or "small" are usually derogatory. Particularly troublesome are categories of darkness or blackness, which can be latent put-downs of black people. There is a constant need for sensitivity to linguistic forms of prejudice in the rites for the sacraments.

Another form of affirmation of other cultures is in encouraging use of their language. As we have seen, individuals often give themselves to others through words; cultures do no less. Thus, when 28 percent of American Roman Catholics are now Hispanic in origin, justice would seem to be better served if most priests were equipped to celebrate the sacraments in Spanish. And the time is past for the major Protestant denominations to think of themselves as exclusively English-speaking bodies. The United Methodist

Church has two Annual Conferences of Spanish-speaking Christians.

Words and actions are both necessary for sacraments. Yet, the use of rites and ceremonial inevitably produces the dangers of creating or reinforcing injustices. The Church is hardly in a position to be a leaven for society if it is involved in injustice in its sacraments. Such problems both weaken faith and demean the lives of devout Christians. To be told or shown weekly that one is inferior, of less value than others, to be the victim of racism, sexism, ageism, or clericalism, even in church, is certainly a perversion of God's self giving accomplished through human hands and mouths in the sacraments.

Our alternative is constant vigilance that in our actions and words we heed the demands for justice within the Church. A continuous scrutiny of our sacramental practices is necessary to be certain that they do not, even unwittingly, become prejudicial, exclusive, or discriminatory. At best, the sacraments are powerful forces for justice. Only when diverted through loss of concern for the full human worth of all others do they become forces for injustice. Here, too, it is well to remember our baptism.

IV

We have seen that baptism initiates us into a community based on equality in receiving God's self giving. But within that community the search for justice continues, even as the sacraments can become means of oppression as well as forces for righteousness. Now we turn to look at the mission of sacraments to the world. Christians have been tempted in every age to regard the sacraments as entirely internal within the Church, as if their influence reached no farther than the church door. But the sacraments do have a profound external impact on society. Indeed, the Church's impact on the world is largely shaped by its sacramental life. This is particularly true of the eucharist and of reconciliation, both of which have had, and continue to have, a profound effect on the world's struggle for justice.

The sacraments' contribution to the battle for justice is contained in the term "persistence." Baptism is, once and for all, initiating us into the Christian life. But the other dimension of the sacramental life is continuity. Eucharist and reconciliation are lifelong requisites for every Christian. They correspond to needs we never outlive, never outgrow. Our entire life as Christians is a receiving of what God gives through word and sacrament.

It is on this basis that Christians have a contribution to make for justice in the world. Christians can give of themselves because they experience God's self giving. The new United Methodist communion rite states this in the post-communion prayer:

> You have given yourself to us, Lord.
> **Now we give ourselves for others.**
> Your love has made us a new people:
> **As a people of love we will serve you with joy.**
> Your glory has filled our hearts;
> **help us to glorify you in all things.**
> Amen. [8]

Because Christians experience God's self giving in the sacraments, they can give themselves for others.

The Church's contribution to social justice derives largely from its power of making God's love visible in the world through the sacraments. That visibility is a constant need for any Christian's lifelong growth, shaped and transformed by God's acts.

Persistence is essential for efforts for justice. Those who have been involved in political campaigns know that persistence is crucial. One does not transform society with short-term campaigns. When one enlists in a fight for justice, one enlists for a lengthy battle. The powers of evil are too strong, the rewards for wrong too lucrative to readily concede to single setbacks. Injustice is persistent, too, and only yields to greater persistence. The sacraments provide strong rations to enable Christians to "hang in there" in the combat with evil.

The constantly recurring experience of God's self giving in the eucharist and in reconciliation is the Christian's basic source of strength in engaging the world with confidence. For he or she discovers that human self giving in resisting injustice is always more than replenished with that love of God made visible in sacraments. Thus, Christians can "fight the good fight" with enduring strength because they know that once each week they will regroup to give thanks or to ask forgiveness. Efforts for justice will go on as long as we live, but so will the eucharist and reconciliation. And so we can continue. God is eternally persistent, and so we can be in our time.

The eucharist, as we have seen, is a source of God's self giving experienced in a variety of ways. It reminds us most clearly that God acted in human history to give God's only Son in sacrificial love. We can experience that event in the eucharist daily, weekly, or monthly as the divine love that can overcome the world is represented. We constantly need to remember, recall, experience anew that love. Just as we are about to forget the need to give ourselves for others, the eucharist comes around to remind us that God has given Godself for us.

The experience of that divine self giving is our only hope for doing what is good and just. We do good to others because God first loved us, and we perceive that love through word and sacraments. Without the experience of that divine love, we act only to our selfish advantage. Because we experience that love freely given, we can give our love freely. Sacraments set us free from obsession with self so we can give of ourselves.

The love we give to others, because we have been recipients of divine love, is directed to society as well as toward individuals. It is shaped by our understanding of social justice as one form such love takes. The love the eucharist liberates is love that is expressed in mission to establish a more just social order.

Part of the power for justice in the eucharist is its eschatological dimension. Far from being pie-in-the-sky escapism, the eucharist is a foretaste of that just Kingdom where all will be accorded their due. The eucharist was such a revolutionary force in the early Church that virtually, by itself, it could see Christians through the worst forms of persecution. Perhaps this is also why respectable Christendom tended to forget the eschatological elements in the eucharist and to settle for a fitful peace on earth instead of heralding a Kingdom based on justice for all. Modern reforms have highlighted once again words that remind us the eucharist always points beyond to a reality not yet realized. Christ's coming in final victory, our eating a foretaste of the final messianic banquet, the "fulfilment in the kingdom of God" (Luke 22:16) of what we do now on earth are all phrases reminding us of the incompleteness of our present social order. Thus, the eucharist can never be seen as a sanction for the existing social order or for any present economic system.

Jean-Jacques Von Allmen suggests that Christian worship is always a threat to the world, for it calls the world into judgment.[9] At the same time, such worship stands as a beacon of hope for a just order that is not yet come into being. Christians can never rest content with present social conditions, for the eucharist always calls those conditions into judgment. Yet, at the same time, the eucharist gives a word of promise that God wills a most just order.

Thus, the eucharist is both a source of power for the Christian to change society and a condemnation of false confidence in any existing society inasmuch as it falls short of that Kingdom God wills to bring about. The eucharist promises a much more radical vision for humanity than any social reformer has hoped to bring about through the dictatorship of the proletariat, laissez-faire capitalism, or any other purely human panacea. And, unlike these human means, the eucharist also gives power to work toward justice.

Tissa Balasuriya, writing from Sri Lanka in the aftermath of a long period of colonialism, angrily questions how both the oppressed and oppressors can share at the Lord's table.[10] It is a question that cannot be evaded but may be given a proximate answer. All those who share in the Lord's supper are sinners who stand under judgment. The Lord's self giving is not forced upon us; we can accept it gladly and respond in love toward others. But it does not coerce us to change and frequently fails to make us recognize our evil. Both oppressor and oppressed develop ways of manipulating each other even though with unequal resources. The development of defiant hate and anger to the oppressor reduces him or her to less than full humanity. The wish to kill is as damnable as the power to do it (Matt. 5:22).

Those who share in the eucharist certainly continue to sin. But they have greater resources for change, having received the supreme sign-act of gracious self giving and being witnesses to the reign of God built on justice. All are reminded that they stand equally dependent as recipients of God's love. In their ultimate dimension, all are seen as equals and are under obligation to God's law to act accordingly. This does not guarantee they will in most cases. For many of us, the most democratic act of the week is lining up for communion, never knowing beside whom we shall kneel, but realizing that we are all equal at the communion rail. Here all are beggars, as the *Book of Common Prayer* says, "not worthy so much as to gather up the crumbs under thy Table." This recurring rite of equality has more power to overcome inequities than anything else in our society. At the communion rail, we are all equally recipients of the love of God and the only appropriate response is gratitude for all we are and have. Paul had to remind the church in Corinth they shared as equals at the Lord's table and that if they failed to discern Christ's body in their midst they were, instead, eating and drinking judgment on themselves (I Cor. 11:29).

The perception of ourselves as receivers of all we have also applies to the whole created universe. Early and Eastern liturgies stressed God's work of creation as a major part of that for which Christians give thanks when they make eucharist. Unfortunately, this dropped out in the West, and God's work of creation was not mentioned in the eucharistic prayer. It is tempting to speculate how Western culture might have evolved with a less exploitive attitude toward nature had Christians in the West continued to thank God for creation as well as redemption during the last thousand years. The new liturgies all fill this lacuna belatedly. Once again, the eucharist can help us remember that all environmental decisions are moral issues as Christians act in a universe they recognize as God's handiwork.

The eucharist is central in the Church's commitment to social justice as a source of mission and as a witness to the demand for justice in the world. But it is not our only source of action. Every Christian, no matter how devoted to social justice, falls short of the reality for which one strives. Our failures make the sacrament of reconciliation a necessity; God's work of reconciliation makes this sacrament a continuing source of renewal. In it, we experience the possibility of overcoming failure and know others have similar respites.

Since we live in an imperfect world, still under the dominion of sin, we need to be able to cope with our own lapses. The Kingdom, obviously, is not here yet, and we are involved in the sin of our nation, local community, and church. Thus, we often find ourselves ensnared in structures of sin over which we have no control. We may find ourselves constrained to pay taxes for a war we regard as unjust, working for a political party whose stand on some issues is blatantly racist, or forced to make business decisions that exploit the poor. In each case, we discover that we live under the dominion of sin in the social order as well as in our private lives. While striving to be just, we cannot avoid a sense of guilt because of the society we live in. Even the Church, as we have just indicated, can find its sacraments reinforcing unjust structures.

Reconciliation reminds us that God acts not to condemn us but to forgive. Through our examination of conscience, we recognize our participation in structures and individual acts of injustice. Through our act of confession, we articulate our guilt and frustration in our own incapacity to overcome evil. But, through God's word of pardon, we are liberated from the burden of guilt and enabled to return to the front lines in combat with evil. Reconciliation is God's word of forgiveness liberating us to live free of guilt. It is a way of experiencing God's forgiveness in a way to overcome despair. Without such relief, without the constant reassurance that ultimately everything depends upon God, not upon us, we would soon give up. Thus reconciliation provides rest and recreation for the battle-weary Christian.

As with the eucharist, we never outlive or outgrow our need for reconciliation. Saints and sinners alike need to hear that forgiving word, which humans utter in God's name. Reconciliation is essential in developing Christian persistence. Without it, we are only short-term militia, doomed to slink away in discouragement. But, because of reconciliation, we can enlist for a duration that lasts out our lifetime.

Sacraments, then, are an essential part in the Church's campaign for justice, both within its own life, and in the world in which it lives. Through sacraments, the Church itself can be a model of a society truly just, which anticipates a Kingdom based on justice for all. But, even within the Church, there is an ambiguity in the sacraments, a constant danger that they may be misused as vehicles of oppression of groups who are without power to prevent such abuse. Constant scrutiny is necessary even within the Church. A church that has attained ecclesial justice is best equipped to work for justice in society itself. Then, through their own experience of equality in receiving from God, Christians can go forth to join men and women of goodwill to work for a just world order. Because of what they receive in the sacraments, Christians can give themselves in seeking justice for others.

6

*The Reform of
Sacramental Practice*

Sacraments are sources of immense power for building up and sustaining the body of Christ. Through the sacraments, Christians are built up in faith and love, healed in mind and body, enabled to overcome alienation, and equipped to serve others. The community of faith experiences God's self giving in the sacraments in a variety of ways. This enables its members to give themselves to others because of the divine love they have experienced.

All forms of Christian ministry—general (lay people) and representative (ordained clergy)—are based on this fact that Christians minister on the basis of what they have received. The cup of cold water or the counseling word are grounded in love made audible and visible in the worshiping congregation. These acts of love are intrinsically communal in source though they may occur along some remote highway or in some private office or home. Christians are able to give of themselves individually on such occasions because of what they have received communally.

Since sacraments are the source of so much power within the life of the community and in its mission to the world, it is constantly necessary that sacrament practices be scrutinized to see that the most effective use possible is made of the sacraments. This necessitates constant reexamination of practices, both in the light of Christian belief, and in terms of our knowledge of humanity. In our time, such concern has produced a major reformation of practices among both Roman Catholics and Protestants. The reforms emanating from Vatican II among Roman Catholics have been well publicized and, according to public opinion polls, well received by the majority of laity. Reforms under way among Anglicans, Lutherans, and other Protestants have been almost as sweeping, but often have gone unheralded in their progress.

We turn now to surveying the basis on which these reforms are being conceived and implemented. Only then can we discuss the nuts and bolts of the most effective forms of sacramental practice. We now apply what we have learned from observation of the sacraments to critical reflection on how to make more effective the sacramental practices themselves.

I

All Christians, by baptism, are committed to care for each other. The Church, like a body, cannot neglect the well-being of any of its members: "The eye cannot say to the hand, 'I do not need you'; nor the head to the feet, 'I do not need you'" (I Cor. 12:21). Each has a ministry to insure the other's health, though in ways differing according to respective gifts.

All Christians, through their baptism, share in Christ's priestly ministry, the ministry of mediating God's love to others. The general ministry of the baptized includes a ministry of sacraments shared with ordained ministers. Even though certain roles may be reserved in some churches for ordained ministers, all sacraments require the active participation of the general ministry as Christians minister to each other. Sacraments without laity are an anomaly. Some sacraments, such as baptism or marriage, do not require clergy at all. The baptized ministry is the context in which all sacraments are celebrated.

The reformers were anxious to recover these insights and practices. At times, Luther tended to regard clergy as quite dispensable though, in practice, he relied on ordained ministers for conduct of the sacraments. The "priesthood of all believers" came to be a favorite slogan, if not reality, for the Reformation. Frequently, this term implied an attack on clericalism, a leveling down, more than a boost for the laity, a leveling up. But it was a strong effort to witness to the need for all Christians to minister to each other in Christ's name.

Christians are still far from realizing the full impact of the concept of the priesthood of all believers. Some important recent advances in this area have come within post-Vatican II Roman Catholicism. The role of the laity in the *Rite of Christian Initiation of Adults* is essential. Through the ministry of the whole community of faith, as well as individual sponsors, new Christians are led through the process of conversion. Roman Catholic laity are actively being recruited and trained as special ministers of the eucharist. Not only do they help serve communion at mass but many are engaged on a daily basis in taking communion to the sick and shut-ins. They can vastly extend the parish's ministry to its people by this means.

All Christians have ministerial responsibilities to visit and pray for the sick and injured and also to rejoice with the joyful. Laity also share in the counseling processes that surround Christian initiation, engagement and marriage, and experiences of grief. It is difficult to conceive of baptism, marriage, or Christian burial without the various ministries of lay Christians. Godparents or sponsors represent the whole congregation; the wedding party is a supportive group within a community; and the friends who bring food to a bereaved family are a sign of the care of the wider community of faith.

Many of the responsibilities for planning, preparing for, and conducting the sacraments are entrusted in most churches to ordained ministers. Such work depends upon and complements that of the general ministry. Practices vary from denomination to denomination, but usually the representative ministries have prime responsibilities in the ordination of their coworkers and successors and in summing up the community's faith through the great thanksgiving at the eucharist. Some churches reserve the pronouncement of absolution at reconciliation and the laying on of hands at initiation. Thus, most churches treat ordained clergy as the normal, that is, usual, presiders at the sacraments except in extraordinary circumstances.

There are various reasons for this. The most common is the biblical "let all be done decently and in order" (I Cor. 14:40). A consensus on roles is necessary to have orderly worship. A second reason is that clergy, it is to be hoped, have been trained in the leadership of worship and are expected to have more competence in pastoral liturgy. Ordained ministers are also committed to a representative role in being sensitive to the needs of all their people while, at the same time, linking the local congregation to the faith and life of the whole Church. Most denominations deem these are sufficient reasons for entrusting leadership roles in most sacraments to ordained clergy.

The term "pastor" implies the leadership role in the context of a community of Christians. Indeed, it is hard to conceive of the term "pastor," meaning "shepherd," apart from the related term "congregation" (cum grege), meaning "with flock." There is an important relationship of mutuality between pastor and flock. Contrariwise, the use of the terms "pastor" or "pastoral" in the absence of a congregation seems a contradiction in terms.

At the heart of a pastor's relationship to his or her congregation is the ministry of word and sacraments. This responsibility is basically a communal function performed by the pastor in the midst of the worshiping congregation. Pastoral care is exercised to far more people over the pulpit and altar-table than over the office desk or hospital bed. Counseling of individuals is a vital part of a pastor's work, but even that work occurs in the context of a congregation that gathers for word and sacrament. The worshiping congregation is the context within which pastoral care is done. Hence, the leadership of corporate worship is often referred to as pastoral liturgy since this role is so central for pastoral ministry.

For fifteen centuries, the Church exercised most of its pastoral care through sacraments. Its chief means of helping people was through the ministry of congregation and pastor, acting in concert to build up, reconcile, and heal individuals in need or at times of crisis in their life journey. Josef Jungmann, S.J. wrote: "For centuries, the liturgy, actively celebrated, has been the most important form of pastoral care."[1] For millions of Christians, from birth until death, the Church ministered through the sacramental system, helping people get by with help from their community of faith. Unfortunately, by the late Middle Ages, the sacramental system had become so heavily clericalized the West almost equated church with clergy. The powers of the sacraments had become a clerical monopoly. This is shown vividly in the variety of liturgical books the early Church had used for a variety of ministries. These were gradually assimilated into single volumes for the exclusive use of clergy or members of religious orders: missal, breviary, pontifical, and ritual.

The Reformation repudiated this clericalism by challenging the sacramental system on ecclesiological grounds. A large portion of the "captivity" of the sacraments that Luther fought—especially evident in the restriction of the chalice to the clergy, the understanding of transubstantiation, and distorted sacrificial notions then current—were derived from and supported excessive clericalism. The reformers did not negate the central role of clergy in the sacraments, but they put that function in the context of the total Christian community. Luther is quite content to have sacraments emerge entirely from the laity if a group of Christians are stranded on a desert island without clergy. The sacraments were to be a shared responsibility by the whole community. This came to realization among the Disciples of Christ on the American frontier in the nineteenth century. Among Disciples, even the eucharistic prayer is offered by laity.

There were losses in the Reformation's efforts to give the

sacraments a more adequate ecclesiological framework. In the process, the sacramental system was shattered. Reconciliation as a sign-act of setting one's conscience right before God was virtually abandoned, or rather, it was grafted on to the eucharist making that sacrament even more penitential. The sacrament of healing, already seriously deteriorated into last rites, was abandoned though the human needs it ministered to obviously did not disappear. In Reformed and Free Church traditions, funerals tended to be secularized or omitted. Weddings and ordinations survived the least changed.

The result was that sacramental worship receded from its central place in Roman Catholicism to a marginal role in Protestant worship. That was certainly not what Luther, Calvin, Cranmer, or Wesley anticipated or desired. Declericalizing the sacramental system led instead to displacing the sacraments themselves.

Today we see a new reformation of word and sacrament well under way in much of American Protestantism. No longer is clericalism the chief problem; Roman Catholicism itself has moved away from much of that. Ignorance and indifference about worship seem to be the chief obstacles. The new reformation in Protestant worship seeks to recover a balance of both word and sacrament. Widespread adoption of the lectionary and the consequent return to expository preaching are evidences that there is already a pronounced recovery of emphasis on the centrality of the reading and preaching of God's word in worship. More frequent celebration of the eucharist is the best example of regaining the sacramental side of Christian worship. Greater care in baptismal policies and practices are developing. New concern about the importance of other sacraments as the foundation of pastoral care is also evident. What title future generations will apply to the changes in worship in our time we cannot foretell: reformation, reshaping, re-formation, renewal, revitalization, or recovery are possibilities. The changes reflect all of these.

II

The Church has long recognized the need for guidelines if most effective use is to be made of sacraments. In any human social activity we recognize the value of effective procedure. Rules of order expedite business meetings; courts follow fixed customs in order to achieve justice. Those to whom the Church entrusts responsibility for leading celebrations of the sacraments use these powers to serve on the basis of certain agreed standards: namely, one does not baptize a person repeatedly, one does use water for baptism. Most of these agreed practices have evolved by a long accumulation of experience. Ministers do not start afresh trying to discover how to make sacraments effective. They begin on the basis of the accumulated experience of how the Church has discovered they work best.

Anyone responsible for the administration of sacraments submits to a discipline of how to make best use of them. Far from being a restriction, such discipline sets one free. An artist knows the discipline necessary to master a medium before one can be creative. Until one is thoroughly familiar with what clay does when fired, one is not ready to be creative with ceramics. A discipline for use of the sacraments is likewise necessary to become familiar with the most effective ways of using them. Far from limiting freedom, discipline enables the most creative use. Undisciplined use of the sacraments results in chaos and undercuts the ministry of other pastors.

There are parallels in exegetical preaching. A preacher assumes the discipline of certain conventions in order to do the most effective exegetical preaching. One listens to the entire passage rather than imposing the preacher's own ideas on it; one uses all available linguistic tools to discern what the pericope is actually saying. A conscientious preacher uses commentaries and other books to see how scholarship can illumine the text in question. This is not a limitation on the preacher but a means to help him or her work most effectively for the benefit of all who hear the sermon.

There is always danger that sacramental malpractice may be detrimental to the work of brother or sister pastors. If one does not uphold one's denominational standards of what marriages to preside at under what circumstances, then one undercuts the conscientious pastor who does abide by such a discipline. A minister who abides by strict standards of baptism is betrayed by a neighboring pastor whose practice is lax. A discipline of the sacraments according to commonly accepted standards is necessary to collegiality in ordained ministry.

Some pastors always hesitate to say no to what people request. This may be from fear of being judgmental. Yet one of the best means clergy have of serving people is in helping them discern right from wrong. One cannot make sound ethical or sacramental judgments without clearly thought-out norms. Quite frequently the Church may serve people best by saying no rather than acceding to every wish. T. S. Eliot reminded us that there are times when the Church is tender when we wish it were hard, and hard when we wish it were soft. To know when the Church ought to stand firm and when it should be flexible demands knowledge of and use of norms.

Norms are something like the operator's manual in a car. They come in very handy at times in making informed judgments when decisions are necessary. No one regards the operator's manual as a legalistic document, but one ignores it at great risk. We may joke "when all else fails, read the instructions," but we know that if we read them first they would save us a lot of trouble. The car works best the way the instructions indicate. The sacraments work best within recognized norms.

The complexity of human life frequently makes it necessary for pastors to make decisions about how best to serve individuals and community through sacraments. Rarely are completely ad hoc judgments best in such cases. How do you decide whether a eucharist is appropriate at a certain wedding? How do you determine whether a specific adult is ready for baptism? How do you decide whether to conduct a public service of reconciliation? Norms will not answer any of these questions, but they will help one make better-informed judgments than if left to one's own devices. Thus, norms are a great asset in decision making.

In the past, Roman Catholics tended to treat normative statements formulated in canon law as absolute. One played it safe by playing it by the book. The post-Vatican II era has seen an easing of this juridical and legalistic approach to worship in favor of providing a variety of options with much decision making delegated to the local priest. No longer are seminary worship courses taught as courses in rubrics alone. Yet norms are still provided, which a pastor can rely on when difficult decisions have to be made. An arid rubricism was once a major affliction of Roman Catholic worship; that problem is largely past. Sensitive and creative decisions can now be made locally on the basis of a general norm.

In many Protestant denominations, a situation opposite to that of the old Roman Catholic legalism exists. The situation resembles a time of chaos in Israel's history. "In those days there was no king in Israel and every man did what was right in his own eyes" (Judg. 21:25). Such anarchy was reinforced in American Protestantism by the pragmatism of the nineteenth century and its preference for whatever appeared to work, rather than for historical or theological standards. Pastors simply did what appeared to work for them without raising too many questions as to why. And, conversely, one abandoned whatever did not appear to work with even less concern as to the reasons for its apparent failure. The Free Church tradition increasingly interpreted its freedom as consisting in doing what one pleased rather than in the original sense of being free to obey God's word in ordering worship. Any sense of "ought" or "should" was alien to such a spirit.

Norms for the reform of sacramental practice have to provide for change. As the conditions of life change, the meaningfulness of certain acts changes. At the beginning of this century, some regarded it as a great step forward to use small, individual communion glasses, a step pioneered by a Presbyterian pastor in Rochester, New York. Other changes in practice have come about for theological reasons, such as the celebration of communion facing the people in Roman Catholic churches since Vatican II. Whatever norms we use must be dynamic, able to reflect changes in theological understanding and cultural patterns.

We shall consider three general norms as the bases for suggesting reforms in sacramental practice. The general norms deal with pastoral, theological, and historical concerns.[2] Problems in each of these areas affect all decisions for action. If one encounters serious problems in any one of these areas, it is time to reconsider before proceeding. One can imagine a triangle with checkpoints at each angle. A course of action seems desirable if it can pass inspection at each of the three checkpoints: pastoral, theological, and historical. If so, then one is free to proceed. But if halted at any one angle, then the practice should be reconsidered.

The pastoral norm is that *worship must be shaped to fit the needs of actual people in a specific time and place*. An intimate knowledge of one's people is demanded of each pastor so that one will be sensitive as to how the people understand worship practices. Not only does it mean knowing one's people but also accepting and respecting the culture in which they feel comfortable. Their musical tastes, for instance, are not something to be "improved" without further thought. Above all, pastors are called to love their people as they actually are.

This is not as easy as it may sound because university-educated clergy have developed, often unaware, a clerical culture. It may be possible for them to know their people well, but it may be much harder for them to affirm the peoples' culture. This is only possible when one loves them as they are and can resist the temptation to replicate one's own culture in them. Aesthetically this may sound like pure philistinism, as if anything goes. But there are grounds for discrimination within any culture. There is, for example, a variety in what people can and will sing at any level of musical accomplishment.

The pastoral aspect of decision making involves the insights of the human sciences. Not only are aesthetics very important at this point, but also the findings of sociology, cultural anthropology, communications theory, and developmental psychology. Our concern is how members of a specific congregation express and perceive what is ultimately real for them. To understand this, we need the insights of the human sciences.[3]

It is at this point that we are most directly concerned with the quality of celebration. If much of the power of the sacraments lies in their ability to signify God's self giving, then it is essential they be celebrated to achieve the maximum amount of communication. When we discuss quality, we recognize differences in people and their varying ways of perceiving. What communicates in the South Bronx and what communicates a few miles away on Park Avenue may be far removed. The pastoral norm for conceiving reforms has a situational quality that is essential for determining what is most effective in a given context.

The theological norm for sacramental action is that *what we do must reflect Christian faith*. It would make little sense to develop forms of expression that conflicted with essential Christian beliefs. This is an especially sensitive area. Not only is there much diversity of doctrine within Christianity, but also this applies to sacramental doctrine itself. We are not called to reduce the sacraments to any partisan proof-texting. Rather, we are under a mandate to let them reflect central Christian truths that, in many cases, are less subject to controversy than more peripheral ones.

The method we have adopted in this book is to move from the sacraments themselves to Christian theology. The actions of the sacraments tell us much of what we want to know about what Christians believe. In this sense, what Christians do provides an indicator of what Christians believe.

But that in itself is not sufficient. One has to consider what these actions have meant to Christians as they try to reduce them to words. As we have seen, the New Testament writers wrestled with such problems and produced images that have resonated throughout Christian history.

The development of systematic theology cannot be ignored, especially the ironing out of the great Trinitarian and Christological themes in the fourth and fifth centuries. For modern liturgical renewal, recovery of the sense of the distinctive actions of each member of the Trinity has been crucial. Recent explorations of soteriology, eschatology, ecclesiology, and other dimensions of Christian belief have direct bearing on the shape of the sacraments. Thus there is renewed interest in the eschatological dimensions of the eucharist, baptism, and marriage.

Ultimately, sacraments reflect our understanding of how God works in this world. At the theological checkpoint, questions are raised as to whether any contemplated action accords with the way Christians generally perceive the work of God. If not, if, say an action implied the absence or disinterest of God, it would not pass that checkpoint. In raising the question of what is the appropriate action, we can never bypass theological scrutiny to see if it agrees with the main body of Christian belief.

The historical norm is that *we cannot make decisions independently from the worship experiences of millions of Christians around the world over the course of twenty centuries.* The sacramental practices and faith of so many people are too important to ignore. At the lowest level, what has been done and discarded can tell us what is not likely to be feasible in our time either. The price of not knowing history is to have to repeat it. A practice abandoned centuries ago, such as drinking communion wine through straws, is not likely to be worth trying again.

But, at the highest level, the use of history is indeed a most liberating tool. History can expand our knowledge of what is constant in Christian worship and can indicate a diversity of ways those constants can be expressed. Amid such an array of times and places, we must distinguish matters that are culturally conditioned from matters that are of permanent character. It would not seem natural in most cultures to carry the eucharistic bread and wine on top of one's head, though that might be most natural in some African cultures. Yet, the fact that so many cultures include an offertory procession of some sort cannot be ignored as a witness to an action of importance.

Knowledge of history can set us free from our own cultural captivity so we can glimpse or invent other possibilities that might prove most meaningful in our circumstances. Without such knowledge, we are captive to the familiar. With such knowledge, we can transcend our own limitations. The continuity of the human situation makes much that is meaningful for diverse people also available for us. History helps us to discern what is essential so we can expend our creative efforts where they are most fruitful.

123

Furthermore, every portion of Christianity needs the witness of the larger Church. The ecumenical movement has taught us that no denomination is an island. Every congregation, every denomination, needs the larger witness of the total Church. "All that is true, all that is noble, all that is just and pure, all that is lovable and gracious, whatever is excellent and admirable" (Phil. 4:8) is ours to share. Denominational traditions have become extremely eclectic today as each church appropriates from others "whatever is excellent and admirable."

This does not mean that local traditions are overwhelmed. It means quite the opposite. Those churches that do baptize infants need to consider the experience and rationale of those churches that refuse such practice and vice versa. The universal Church is enriched through the experience of particular churches. Many practices that we propose are already widely experienced, such as anointing the sick by the Church of the Brethren. Knowledge of past and current history is a major resource for reformation of our own actions.

We shall conclude this chapter with proposals of thirty-five specific reforms on planning, preparing for, and conducting the sacraments. We shall try to indicate the direction of current efforts at reformation of word and sacrament in the main-line Protestant churches of America. Those reforms we propose are not necessarily existing practice in any denomination. Rather, we propose what should become current practice on the basis of our general norms.

These reforms are proposed as means of initiating changes, where needed, and of provoking discussion in any case. Our practices need constant reassessment. These reforms are based on the threefold general norms mentioned above—pastoral, theological, and historical—though there is not sufficient space for a full-scale defense of each one. Sometimes that will not seem necessary, though in each case, we believe it is possible. Each reform should be capable of passing all three checkpoints.

In proposing these reforms of sacramental practice, we are striving to find better ways of exercising pastoral care of our people. Some reforms will be more relevant in some denominations than in others because of diversity of practices. This cannot be avoided in a book that addresses traditions from Pentecostal to Anglican. The common factor is the desire to find better ways of serving people by providing improved pastoral leadership of worship. If these reforms contribute to that end, they will be well worth proposing.

124

III

Our first three reforms deal with sacraments in general. Then, we shall proceed to the rites of initiation and the other sacraments in turn.

1. *Sacraments should be understood as sign-acts in which God acts anew to give Godself to human beings through words and actions spoken and performed in community.* Unless sacraments are regarded as far more than just pious aids to remember past events, genuine reform of sacramental practice is impossible. We need not reiterate what has already been said on this subject except to insist that this reform is basic for all that follows. But this is a radical step for many Protestants who have been so desacralized that for them to consider sacraments as divine acts represents a major change.

2. *In all sacraments, careful attention must be given to achieving the full sign value of what is being signified.* The quality of celebration is a major pastoral concern in making God's love visible through celebrations of the sacraments. The "outward and visible" is not contrasted to the "inward and spiritual"; both are different aspects of the same reality. Essentially, outward and inward or visible and spiritual are one and the same. We do not distinguish between human love and the expressions of it. No more should we make distinctions between God's love and manifestations of it. Indifference to the visible and tangible aspects of worship does not make it more spiritual but frequently lessens its efficacy for worshipers.

3. *Sacramental practice must always be subject to scrutiny lest words, actions, or roles employed become sources of injustice to some.* Stated in a more positive fashion, sacraments must be seen as opportunities for affirming the equal rights of all as recipients of God's self giving and as means of equipping Christians for mission in creating a more just society outside the Church. Sacraments are change agents within the Church and in the world beyond. There is always danger that the Church may overlook the beam in its own eye and perform the sacraments in ways that are demeaning to some of its own members. Vigilance is necessary to insure justice within the Church. Sacraments enable Christians to work for justice in the world.

4. *Baptism should be performed only when there is adequate counseling and instruction of candidates or their parents.* This is essential for the reform of baptismal practice. Baptism is so important that it should not occur without adequate preparation of

the candidates, or the parents in the case of infants. The early Church could require as long as three years of preparation for baptism. It cannot be assumed that parents are aware of what responsibilities they are undertaking for an infant or child. Nor can it be taken for granted that every youth or adult who requests baptism senses the ethical and creedal changes that, this act demands.

Parents may be surprised to learn what responsibilities they are assuming when presenting a child for baptism. They may even decline baptism when they discover what it entails. This is better than to make baptism a meaningless baby launching. When parents have been counseled as to what is expected and they decline, they and the Church both keep their integrity far more than when baptism is just a pro forma affair.

5. *Baptism of an infant should be practiced only when the parent or parents are professed Christians who promise to rear the child in an environment of faith.* An exception might be made for a baby when someone promises to be a sponsor as surrogate for the parents. This is problematic, given the mobility of American society. There is no reason to continue indiscriminate ("promiscuous") baptism of all children with little likelihood of many being brought to faith. Should parents become practicing Christians, baptism is always possible for their children at a later date. Baptizing without the likelihood of faith development makes baptism little more than a magical act, a talisman for protection. Baptism always demands commitment, either from candidates or from someone responsible to lead them in maturing in faith.

6. *The unity of Christian initiation should be restored so that baptism, laying on of hands (or anointing), and first communion come at the same time, no matter at what age.* This has been the practice of the Orthodox and Oriental churches throughout history and was that of the West as late as the twelfth century. When God acts to incorporate us into the body of Christ, it is not a halfway gesture with portions deferred to a later date. In the case of youth and adults, it is already usual for initiation to be complete at one time; infants and small children should be treated likewise. An integrated rite stresses God's activity, not ours. This integration is provided for in the new Lutheran, Episcopal, and United Methodist rites.

7. *Baptism should be renewed or reaffirmed regularly throughout life.* What God has done in our baptism ought to be recalled with thanksgiving throughout life. As we continue life's journey, we develop as persons—the same, yet different. We need periodic

rediscovery of fresh meaning in our baptism. A rite for this is part of the celebration of the paschal vigil for Roman Catholics and can be celebrated at Easter or other times in the new Lutheran, Episcopal, and United Methodist rites. The visual presence of the baptismal font, or baptistry, is also a continual reminder of baptism.

8. *Baptism itself should never be repeated.* God's promise to us is sure no matter how tenuous our response to it may be. Repetition of baptism suggests that God was lying to us. If there is any doubt whether baptism actually occurred, conditional baptism can be performed. It is prefaced by the words: "If you are not already baptized, I baptize you . . ." Renewal or reaffirmation of baptism is not repetition but thankful recalling of what God did for us in baptism.

9. *Baptism should always be a public event in the midst of a worshiping community.* The presence of a community of faith is almost as important as the use of water. Baptism is always into a community and the presence and participation of that community is a basic part of the sign-act. It is difficult to signify becoming part of "a people claimed by God for his own" (I Pet. 2:9) if that people is absent. The community also rediscovers its basis for being as it experiences anew its own creation through baptism.

10. *Baptisms should normally occur in baptismal festivals at special times during the liturgical year.* This practice, advocated in the new Lutheran reforms, ties baptism into the ongoing remembrance of God's acts in Jesus Christ. It helps make baptism not just an occasional event but an integral part of the whole Christian mystery. Events especially recommended are: the Baptism of the Lord (recalling Jesus' own baptism), the Paschal Vigil (the most solemn occasion for baptism as the resurrection is celebrated), Pentecost Day (commemorating the birth of the Church), and All Saints' Day (remembering Christ's work in the Church throughout time). At these times, special hymns, banners, and other visuals are appropriate.

11. *The full sign value of the cleansing power of baptism should be manifest.* The washing power of water is the most obvious liturgical sign present, yet it often becomes so minimalized that many baptisms appear to be dry cleaning. Generous use of water, whatever the mode used, helps testify to God's saving action in which we are washed clean of sin purely by God's generous act of forgiveness. Immersion is the most powerful sign of this. Dipping or submersion is being used increasingly for infants as it was in the West until recent centuries. Failing that, pouring can be a demonstrative act. Sprinkling or mere moistening are much too

minimal to be effective signs. Obviously, adequate fonts are necessary, with a basin at least two feet in diameter; mere candy dishes will not do. The water should be seen, heard, and indirectly felt by all present. Something happens in baptism; it is not merely described. This is obvious in immersions; it should be made more so in all baptisms as we become sensitive to how human beings communicate.

12. *The eucharist should be celebrated as the main service in local churches each Sunday.* This would not seem remarkable for Churches of Christ, Disciples of Christ, Roman Catholic, and Orthodox Christians. But, as argued in chapter 3, the recovery of a weekly eucharist is the highest priority for the reform of worship in most Protestant churches.

Nevertheless, it must be said distinctly that to institute a weekly celebration of the eucharist under the spirit and form in which it is now performed monthly or occasionally in most Protestant churches would be an unmitigated disaster. As usually celebrated (if that is, indeed, the proper term), it is unduly long, unduly lugubrious, and unduly penitential. Hence, careful rethinking of the meaning of the eucharist and thorough restructuring of the way it is celebrated is essential. In most cases, the significance of the eucharistic prayer especially needs study and the method of distributing communion particularly demands retooling. Much other work must be accomplished before a recovery of a weekly eucharist would be beneficial. It is hoped that the specific reforms that follow will point essential directions.

13. *The eucharist should always include the reading and preaching of God's word.* The reformers seem unanimous on this; word and sacrament belong together. Both are at their best when united; both suffer when put asunder. This does not mean a so-called "communion meditation" is desirable, but rather an exposition of a biblical text from the regular course of readings. God's word should be both proclaimed and enacted at each eucharist.

14. *The eucharist should be celebrated so that the important actions have the highest possible sign value.* Actions, when carefully done, can communicate as much or more than words. It is a good learning experience to celebrate the eucharist without any spoken words or music in order to discover how much, especially the verbs, can be communicated by actions. The fourfold actions of taking, blessing, breaking, and giving are central, but there are numerous subsidiary actions that communicate. The way one handles the Bible says much about its meaning or insignificance in

one's theology. The same is true of the handling of the bread and wine. Do we actually give the bread as a gift, touching the hand of each recipient, or is it simply grabbed and all enactment of giving missed? Laity can be trained to distribute the elements so that the sense of giving is communicated. Breaking the bread is also a most meaningful act when carefully done.

15. *The eucharistic prayer, spoken by a designated person or persons, should sum up in thanksgiving the center of the community's life together.* In most denominations, an ordained elder, presbyter, or priest proclaims the eucharistic prayer on the basis of that one's ordination, theological training, and knowledge of and love for the people gathered. It is that one's most important function as a pastoral theologian. The faith of the community must be articulated and proclamation made of those acts of God for which the community gives thanks and to which it owes its very existence. This faith the presider proclaims as representative minister. The people add their assent through acclamations and the amen. Recent studies have made clear the inadequacies of the eucharistic prayers of Middle Ages and Reformation alike. One could say that when a seminarian can compose an adequate eucharistic prayer for a given congregation and occasion, that person may be ready for graduation.

16. *Communion should be open to all baptized Christians.* In some churches, baptized children are excluded. Some denominations exclude baptized Christians of other denominations or congregations. Unbaptized people should be encouraged to prepare for and present themselves first for baptism and then eucharist. It is not a service to them to welcome them to the Lord's table without the ethical and creedal commitment demanded of other Christians or of their parents.

17. *The eucharist should be celebrated facing the people with the altar-table as visible and as close to them as possible.* It is amazing to find that in many Protestant churches the minister follows the medieval pattern of celebrating with his or her back to the congregation as if God were remote from the people rather than present among them. Since 1965, Roman Catholic altar-tables have been moved or replaced so the priest faces the assembly. If the altar-table is too low, say thirty inches high as in many Protestant churches where the minister hitherto knelt before it, it may need to be replaced by one of standard height (thirty-nine inches). Its height is more nearly like a kitchen counter where one stands than a table where one sits.

Once one has celebrated facing the assembly, it is difficult to conceive of ever again wanting to turn one's back on the family of God. Being close enough literally and symbolically to reach out and touch one's people is a major step toward emphasizing the fellowship of the gathered community. The architectural setting may do far more to shape peoples' understanding of the nature of the Christian community than a sermon on our equality in Christ. If the building contradicts the sermon, the building is more likely to win.

18. *Real elements of bread and wine should be used.* Substitutes, such as tasteless wafers or cubes, bland grape juice, or even artificial products, are obvious evasions of the biblical witness and make the Lord's supper into denominational enclaves rather than ecumenical feasts. Grape juice is a relatively modern invention (first recommended for Methodists in the 1876 *Discipline*). Tasteless wafers may have been used longer, but the use of "the best and purest wheate bread that conueniently maye be gotten" that the 1552 *Book of Common Prayer* enjoined would be much better. Phony bread and wine contradict our words and actions and are barriers to unity.

19. *A common chalice and a loaf of actual bread should be restored.* The sign value of the unity of the Church achieved through sharing from a common chalice and a single loaf of bread (I Cor. 10:16-17) is too powerful to neglect. When care is used with the common chalice (turning and wiping it), there seems to be less danger of infection than from breathing the air in church. Few people are deterred from attending church because of breathing common air. The loaf should be broken as a significant act in the service. The sign value is considerably increased when a single loaf is broken and used. Only a limited number of people should break and handle it. Complaints are legitimate when a loaf of bread is passed from hand to hand. When only the minister and those assisting handle the bread, there seems to be little reason for objection.

20. *The communicants should leave their pews and receive the elements while sitting at tables, standing, or kneeling.* The act of moving forward in the company of one's fellow Christians is one of the most eloquent acts of the service. Nothing is gained from having all receive at the same time, apparently the only argument for pew communion. Much is gained from common movement to assemble about a table, communion station, or communion rail. The method becoming most common in many churches is that of receiving communion, while standing, from ministers and assistants at several communion stations at the head of each aisle.

Those receiving it then kneel at the communion rail as long as they wish or return immediately to their seats. Nothing detracts from the service more than "table dismissals." Elimination of these reduces the length of the service and ends fracturing the congregation. Congregational song throughout the time of distribution is much to be preferred to the subjective and individualistic devotions encouraged by silence, choral music, or organ background music. The warmth and corporateness stimulated by congregational song at this point in the service provides the best single opportunity to celebrate with joy God's self giving.

21. *Ordination should center in the laying on of hands in the context of prayer which invokes the pouring out of the Holy Spirit.* This central act in ordination has, since medieval times, been obscured by peripheral acts such as the giving of instruments of ministry. The key words also tended to be an imperative statement rather than prayer invoking the outpouring of the Spirit. Many denominations today are recovering similar versions of the central prayer. They have many parallels to the eucharistic prayer. God's past acts in providing leadership are commemorated, and present action is sought in giving necessary gifts to those now being ordained.

22. *Reordination of people transferring to another denomination or resuming active ordained ministry should not be practiced.* There is enormous diversity within Protestantism as to the forms ordination may take, the name of the order or office to which ordination admits, and the positions of those who perform the ordination. In some cases, one still remains a layperson after ordination. In other cases, laity may ordain clergy. When clergy are ordained by other clergy, some way of recognizing their orders among other churches should be developed. In cases where clergy have been ordained by laity, these orders, too, might be acceptable to many churches. If the role of minister has simply been assumed or ordination was to an office regarded as lay, it should be possible to ordain without fear of reordination. A person who has left active ministry to sell insurance should not be reordained when returning to church work, though that person's orders might publicly be recognized. Reordination, as with rebaptism, suggests that God's gifts failed or that the ordained ministry of one church is inferior to that of another. There are some positive features in the concept of indelibility (permanence) of baptism and ordination. Ordained ministry is a gift to be exercised, a gift that is not retracted.

23. *Ordination should always be public with both laity and the newly ordained participating in the rite.* It is wrong to think of

ordination as conveying power for individual enhancement or private prestige. Ordination is always for service within community and this can be shown best by having those to be served present. Laity approve those about to be ordained for service to themselves and join in prayer for the ordinands. Those being ordained can exercise their new responsibilities by reading the gospel lesson (deacons) or by joining in leading the eucharistic prayer (presbyters). The Lord's supper is the context in which ordination ought to occur. Laity and clergy alike should participate in communion.

24. *Services of Christian marriage should not be conducted unless there has been adequate counseling as to Christian understanding of marriage.* It can no longer be assumed that all people will have the same understanding of marriage as once was current in a Christian society. Unwillingness to take the time for such counseling may indicate that a couple, even though baptized, are no longer believers. For them, a secular service that does not force them to pretend to be practicing Christians would relieve them of hypocrisy. At the same time, it would free the Church to make its own wedding services more definitely acts of Christian worship. The Church should not appear to condone relationships hastily contracted.

25. *Christian marriage services should be planned as acts of worship.* The availability of secular services for those who do not profess Christian faith allows the possibility of making the weddings of Christians more definitely acts of Christian worship. Hymns, scripture, a sermon, everything customary in worship except the offering (which they have had already), may be included. For many Christian couples, a eucharist would be most appropriate though the nature of the gathered congregation may indicate that this should occur previously for those who can take communion with them.

26. *For Christians, the vows should include the promise of a lifelong intention of commitment to each other.* Though the wording may vary, Christian marriage is intended to be lifelong, not contingent upon "as long as we love each other," or "until someone better comes along." The vows the couple exchange in the presence of witnesses are meant to be a covenant in which God acts as guarantor and witness. Thus, nothing is conditional, nothing is withheld.

27. *The couple should act as celebrants of the wedding.* The minister is present only to guide the process and to bless them in the name of the Church. The couple make each other husband and

wife through the public exchange of vows; no one else should pronounce them husband and wife. It would be best for them to face each other for the vows, thus signifying to whom the vows are made.

28. *Divorce ceremonies should not be conducted by the Church.* The Church has every concern for those who have gone through the agony of a divorce. It recognizes the imperfection of human nature whereby human sin and finitude sometimes makes divorce unavoidable. Occasional services of reconciliation (confession) ought to be available for everyone, including those who have come close to, or experienced, the breakdown of the marriage covenant. These would remind all of God's will to forgive rather than to condemn. Divorce is not as an inevitable passage as death. It would be hard to see in it an event of God's self giving.

29. *Churches should have occasional public services of reconciliation.* There is need for public occasions in which all Christians confess their sins and hear forgiveness proclaimed. All have transgressed both as individuals and corporately. Even the Church needs to confess its corporate guilt. We need something far more probing than a general confession at the beginning of a weekly service and an absolution more emphatic than a quick word of pardon. Quarterly services of reconciliation (as often as many churches once observed communion) could confront us with God's word, engage us in introspective examination of conscience, lead us to confess our sin, and give assurance of God's will to forgive. Such services would allow the eucharist to be more frequent and free it of its penitential baggage.

30. *All Christians can exercise their priestly ministry in pronouncing forgiveness in God's name to penitents.* Whether it would be wise to confess to some people is dubious, especially when one's neighbor may not abide by confidentiality. The power to declare God's forgiveness should be seen as power conferred on Christians when baptized into Christ's priesthood. It gives each one an important means of ministering to others.

31. *Services of healing ought to be conducted as public services as well as private.* Ministry is to whole persons, not just souls. Thus, God's will to heal ought to be indicated in occasional public services as well as in private services in the sickroom when needed. Healing has much in common with conversion and forgiveness. Reading and preaching of God's word would seem a vital part of healing services as God's love for all creatures is declared.

32. *Services of healing, public or private, ought to include confession and pardon of sin, prayer for healing, and some physical*

act. Healing of the body and healing of the mind are intimately related. Ministry to the whole person is shown in the work of reconciliation. Prayer is important to address our concern to God and to reflect God's concern for us. When we seek physical healing, it is certainly appropriate that some physical act, such as anointing with oil, a handclasp, or a hand laid on the forehead is employed. Frequently this may be the only part of the service a seriously ill person is able to perceive.

33. *Christian burial should be an act of public worship.* Although rites with indefinite character may be provided as a service for nonbelievers, Christian burial ought to be an occasion in which the community of faith joins in worshiping God. Christian burial can include most of the features of a normal service of worship including the eucharist. There is good reason to have the funeral in the church where the deceased worshiped in life, rather than in a commercial chapel. When possible, the body should be present but the casket closed.

34. *Christian burial ought to stress the trustworthiness of God.* Only the strong promises of scripture are sufficient in the face of death. We have to offer not our own word about some doctrine of death but God's own evidence of trustworthiness. Secular poetry or music cannot match the strong affirmations of the biblical lessons and psalms. Congregational participation in prayer and hymnody also testifies best to God's trustworthiness.

35. *Christian burial should be seen as part of a long process of grief ministry.* We minister in the midst of community in the funeral service. The community witnesses to the bereaved in many ways. In supporting the bereaved during the days after the death, the community's role of sympathetic (suffering with) understanding is important. Long after the funeral, the community works to reintegrate the bereaved into its life. On certain anniversaries, such as All Saints' Day and other memorial occasions, the community continues its ministry to the bereaved. From birth to death, God works through the community of faith to give Godself to us in the sacraments.

A Roman Catholic Response

EDWARD J. KILMARTIN, S.J.

During the past few centuries Western Christian theologians have been content to work out systematic theologies of the sacraments from the dogmatic teaching of their respective traditions. The appeal to the teaching of the Council of Trent by Roman Catholic theologians is well known. Lutheran scholars have employed their understanding of the doctrine of justification by faith alone as the basis for sacramental theology. Those of the Calvinist tradition have been influenced to a great extent by Calvin's ecclesiology, which distinguishes rather sharply between the visible and invisible Church, as well as by his pessimistic doctrine of predestination. Modern liturgical scholars have taken a different tack. They are asking: What does the liturgy itself have to say about the meaning of the sacraments? To what extent does its message provide insights that may help to broaden the understanding of the sacraments? Professor White's book offers an example of this liturgical approach.

His analysis of the liturgy of the sacraments yields two general conclusions, which harmonize with the more fruitful contributions of liturgical scholarship to this subject: 1. The unifying concept of all sacramental activity is self giving; 2. Individual sacraments are differentiated in accord with the various human ways in which they express the self giving of God and the liturgical community. From these conclusions a number of interesting theological and pastoral corollaries are formulated.

The limitations of this brief essay do not permit a detailed reply to the whole, or even a substantial part of this work. Rather, it contains a record of some reflections that were prompted by the methodological approach and choice of the motif of self giving, which Professor White understands to be "the most satisfactory thematic element for viewing the use God makes of sacraments."

I. The Sacraments: Expressions of Self Giving

The liturgy of the sacraments is the expression of the worship of the Church. At the same time this liturgy announces that it is a medium of God's self giving. However, this optimistic claim presumes that the authentic faith of the Church is appropriated and expressed by the celebrating community. Only when the participants really worship God in faith does the self giving of God inaugurate or deepen a holy union.

The liturgy also expresses the idea that God's self giving takes place through human means of communication: symbolic word and action. But it does not explicitly teach how the self giving of God through human means of communication relates to the self giving of the community through the same means. Theological reflection on this question has led in two directions. If it can be said that the liturgy involves the believers' self giving *and* God's self giving, there still remains the problem of the interpretation of the "and."

In Western patristic theology this "and" is understood to represent a relationship of dependence. St. Augustine, for example, does not treat it as disjunctive. Rather the "and" serves to indicate a relationship of dependence that is grounded in the divine plan of salvation. He frequently speaks of holy mother Church (*sancta mater ecclesia*) who brings forth children from her womb (baptism) and nourishes them in the eucharist. The holy Church, in union with Christ, is the administrator of the sacraments because of the power of the Holy Spirit that works through her.

On the other hand, the Western patristic notion of the living organism of the holy Church as administrator of the sacraments became somewhat obscured by later theological developments in the West, which tended to support a conceptual separation between the Church as institution of salvation and the Church as holy people of God. In this purview the concept of God's self giving, mediated through human self giving in the sacraments, faded into the background. One result of this was the sharp distinction made between the liturgical rites in which God acts and those in which the community acts.

The Protestant Reformation did little to reverse this tendency. Its weak ecclesiological grounding of the sacraments and the appeal to a word of the historical Christ to establish the authentic sacraments further unraveled the intimate connection between the sacraments and the living organism of the Body of Christ. The popular nineteenth-century American Protestant theology of verbal inspiration of scripture also contributed to this separation. In this theology the "Book of the Bible" is understood to be an institution solely of divine origin, immune from the vicissitudes of the faith of the Church. This outlook corresponds to, and supports, a traditional Protestant understanding of baptism and the eucharist as institutions *in* the Church, originating solely from a word of the historical Christ and functioning independently of the faith of the Church.

In recent times Catholic and Protestant scholars have highlighted the role of the Church in the formation of the New Testament and in the origin of the sacraments. More commonly God's self giving in scripture and in the sacraments is described as mediated by the exercise of the faith of the Church. The New Testament and the sacraments are understood to have come into being through the Church's life of faith. Correspondingly, the efficacy of the preaching of the word of God and the celebrations of the sacraments is seen to be conditioned to some degree by the life of faith of the preacher and the celebrating community.

Professor White seems to agree with this modern outlook. This would explain his view that the quality of the experience of the mystery dimension of worship depends on the quality of the participation of the gathered community. The faith of the whole Church is certainly rendered present in an objective way by the reading of scripture and the employment of the approved liturgy. But the extent to which the concrete community appropriates and manifests this faith as its own contributes significantly to the fruitfulness of the sacramental happening. Pastoral experience confirms this and serves as grounds for the more general theological proposition: God obtains access to the world of human beings as they communicate with one another in faith, hope, and love. Thus, we are led to a theology reminiscent of Augustine's understanding of the role of holy mother Church in the celebration of sacraments.

Professor White's remarks on the quality of the participation of the community prompts this question: How should Christians prepare for the liturgy? The structure of the liturgy and its richness of expression surely contribute much to the quality of participation. But what the participants bring to the celebration of themselves is crucial. The two ways of preparing for the liturgy correspond to the essential elements of the liturgy—prayer and symbolic action. They are social action undertaken in the name of Christ and private prayer.

There is an intimate connection between liturgical worship and

137

social action. The former is an expression of the openness of the creature to God and a means used by God to enter into the heart and mind of the worshiper. Thus the goal of prayer corresponds to the goal of creation: God's self communication to the creature. This openness of the creature to let God be God in one's life has the effect of liberating one from self-seeking and self-justification, from a concern to secure one's self at any price. It gives birth to a confidence that issues in self-forgetful love. Consequently one is moved to extend God's coming to the full range of human activity, to afford space for God's further entrance into the world through one's own self giving.

On the other hand, social action, the caring for others both structurally and personally, can be a source of revitalization of liturgical prayer. If the other, whom one serves, is approached as other—as possessed of inviolable dignity and accessible only by a gracious invitation—this can lead to the recognition of the source of otherness: Our Father. Moreover it will be disclosed that the self giving, which inspires the other to accept his or her otherness, is only a means the Father uses to affirm that this person is really "somebody" of irreducible value. The paradigm of this revelatory function of human self giving is found in the life of Christ. In his human self giving, the Father reveals himself as the basis and goal of all acts of love. As the Fourth Gospel states: "The Word became flesh . . . and we have seen his glory: the glory of an only Son coming from the Father, filled with enduring love . . . Of his fullness we have all had a share—love following upon love" (John 1:14-16 NAB).

The interplay between the liturgical experience of God's self giving as the basis and goal of all human self giving and the experience of the mediation of God's self giving in social action assures the vitality of authentic Christian communal worship and service in the world. However, this experience is scarcely to be expected without a deeply personal life of prayer. On this subject we can only recall a Christian tradition that extends from the early patristic period, down through the Carthusian spiritual exegesis of the Middle Ages, to the present time.

In this tradition it is taken for granted that the same spiritual event that takes place in the liturgy can also be predicated of the attentive reading of scripture and meditation on the life of Christ. Both meditation on scripture and participation in the liturgy are understood as complementary ways of participation in the mystery of God's self giving in Christ from which the knowledge and strength comes to live a life in the service of God's self giving to others.

II. Liturgy as Source of Theology

The relationship between liturgy and theology is expressed by two traditional axioms: 1. law of prayer—law of belief; 2. liturgy—source of theology. These two axioms have been interpreted in different ways. The Modernist G. Tyrrell argued that the prayer of the Church is a measure and norm of its faith. As the more original expression of the faith, it serves as the proving ground for the orthodoxy of any teaching. More often, perhaps, the axiom has been interpreted in a completely opposite way: The official doctrine of the Church determines the law of prayer.

The axiom originates in the *Capitula Coelestini*, a work of Prosper of Aquitaine (d. circa 463). He states that "the law of prayer establishes the law of belief." This is said with reference to the use of petitionary prayer for unbelievers. These prayers prove, against the Semi-Pelagians, that grace is needed for one to take the first step toward conversion. However, it is significant that Prosper grounds the law of prayer on both the conviction of the faith of the Church and the command of Paul expressed in 1 Timothy 2:1-2. Consequently, the liturgical argument is considered valid on two counts: the witness of the New Testament and the tradition of the Church.

The use of the liturgy as source of doctrinal teaching has a long history. Numerous examples can be found in patristic literature. Besides that of the *Capitula Coelestini*, mention can be made of Augustine's appeal to the practice of infant baptism to support his teaching on Original Sin. Throughout the Middle Ages liturgy was also awarded a place among the authorities and sources of doctrinal teaching. Nevertheless, the argument from liturgy was seldom used. During the ensuing period down to the middle of the nineteenth century, systematic theology generally neglected this source. Afterward it was employed as proof texts for dogmatic positions.

In recent times one often hears of the rediscovery of the liturgy by sacramental theology. Numerous articles have been written on this subject, stressing the value of the liturgy as a source for systematic theology. However, the more penetrating studies on this subject are quick to point out that a completely satisfactory approach to the liturgical witness has not been developed. One obvious problem occurs where a liturgical text contains a doctrinal statement and correlative signs derived from the reflex theology of a particular tradition. Other texts are basically determined by the language and customs of a local popular piety that has dubious value for a catholic sacramental theology.

On the positive side, there is agreement among scholars that the ambiguity and openness of the symbolic language and activity of the liturgy have the potential to provide many insights that can contribute to a new systematic theology of the sacraments. The liturgy contains instructional ingredients in its prayer, song, and symbolic actions. But the purpose of this instruction is to awaken faith to action and not precisely to provide doctrinal information. In its characteristic expression the liturgy provides only indirect information about theological implications. It may not be simply reduced to a source of proof texts for dogmatic theology. Therein lies its potential to contribute to a new theology of the sacraments and, in particular, to the ecumenical dialogue between the various Christian traditions.

The ecumenical conversations between the churches over the theology of the sacraments is still bogged down by the playing off of one dogmatic position against the other. The various liturgical traditions, which reflect a more uniform theology, can help to provide an escape from this cul-de-sac. Many a common inheritance, still hidden in the liturgical celebrations of the sacraments, calls for an articulation that can contribute to a new theological orientation. An example of this is Professor White's analysis of the concept of self giving, which is expressed in the sacraments. To the extent that this method of theologizing finds place in the ecumenical dialogues, it may be expected that many doctrinal barriers to the visible unity between Christians will be removed.

Notes

1. The Humanity of the Sacraments

1. For a history of these developments in the 1960s, cf. Joseph Powers, *Eucharistic Theology* (New York: Herder & Herder, 1967), pp. 111-54. An excellent survey of recent contributions of the human sciences appears in George Worgul's *From Magic to Metaphor* (New York: Paulist Press, 1980), pp. 47-120.

2. Victor Paul Furnish, *The Love Command in the New Testament* (Nashville: Abingdon Press, 1972), p. 230.

3. J. L. Austin called this exchange of vows "a performative utterance" in the sense that "the utterance is the performing of an action—it is not normally thought of as just saying something." *How to Do Things with Words* (New York: Oxford University Press, 1965), pp. 6-7.

4. Quoted by Peter Brunner in *Worship in the Name of Jesus* (St. Louis: Concordia Publishing House, 1968), p. 123; (WA XLIX, 588, 15-18).

5. Cf. my "Coming Together in Christ's Name," *Liturgy* I (Fall, 1981): 7-10.

6. "Babylonian Captivity of the Church," *Luther's Works* (Philadelphia: Fortress Press, 1959), XXXVI, p. 62.

7. "Tractus on John," LXXX, 3, *Nicene and Post-Nicene Fathers First Series* (New York: Charles Scribner's Sons, 1908), VII, 344.

8. *Christ the Sacrament of the Encounter with God* (New York: Sheed & Ward, 1963), p. 15. Schillebeeckx's book marks a major landmark in Roman Catholic sacramental theology. He builds upon, although not uncritically, the work of Odo Casel, O.S.B. (1886–1948) whose writings may be sampled in English in *The Mystery of Christian Worship and Other Writings*, edited by Burkhard Neunheuser, translated by I. T. Hale (Westminster, Md.: Newman, 1962).

9. Ibid., p. 45.

10. *Institutes of the Christian Religion IV*, xiv, 3. Edited by John T. McNeill, translated by Ford Lewis Battles. (Philadelphia: The Westminster Press, 1960), p. 1278.

11. *Institutes, IV*, xvii, p. 1361.

12. *Constitution on the Sacred Liturgy*, 7. (Collegeville: Liturgical Press, 1963), p. 9.

13. "Concerning the Order of Public Worship," *Luther's Works* (Philadelphia: Fortress Press, 1965), LIII, p. 11.

14. *Institutes, IV*, xvii, 39, p. 1416.

15. "Of Baptism," *Zwingli and Bullinger*, edited by G. W. Bromiley (Philadelphia: The Westminster Press, 1953), p. 156.

16. Aquinas, *Summa Theologica III*, q. 62, a. 1 (New York: Benziger Brothers, 1947), II, 2356.

141

17. Odo Casel stressed the value of seeing the sacramental life as a sharing in God's saving acts and therefore prior to theological reflection upon them.

18. For a strong statement of this negative aspect of the concept of validity cf. Robert W. Jenson, *Visible Words* (Philadelphia: Fortress Press, 1978), p. 8.

Chapter 2. The Gift of Baptism

1. A. George, "A Literary Catalogue of New Testament Passages on Baptism," in *Baptism in the New Testament* (Baltimore: Helicon Press, 1964), pp. 13-22.

2. Hans Conzelmann speaks of this as an "eschatological abrogation of human differences: in Christ they no longer exist—that is to say, in his body, in the Church." *1 Corinthians;* Hermeneia Commentary (Philadelphia: Fortress Press, 1975), p. 212.

3. James Dunn, *Baptism and the Holy Spirit* (London: SCM Press, 1970) to the contrary.

4. Conzelmann speculates that *epotisthemen* here could be "an allusion to the Lord's Supper," which would seem natural if it was the culmination of the baptismal rite. This would undercut even further attempts to speculate on the moment of the Spirit's conferral, p. 212, n. 17.

5. Charles Wheatly, writing in 1710, speaks of the innovation of sprinkling in the more fashionable churches of London. Cf. his *Rational Illustration* (London: Bohn, 1852), p. 351. John Wesley, in Georgia, in the 1730s, still insisted on observing the prayer book rubric to dip the infant.

6. "The Babylonian Captivity of the Church," *Luther's Works,* XXXVI, 68.

7. Cf. for a detailed account of medieval developments, J. D. C. Fisher, *Christian Initiation: Baptism in the Medieval West* (London: S.P.C.K., 1965).

8. Cf. John G. Davies, *The Architectural Setting of Baptism* (London: Barrie and Rockliff, 1962), pp. 14-17. Davies indicates the enormous variety of visual images shaping baptistries, fonts, and attendant iconography. Cf. also Gilbert Cope, *Symbolism in the Bible and the Church* (London: SCM Press, 1959).

9. "Views of Christian Nurture," in *Horace Bushnell,* edited by H. Shelton Smith. (New York: Oxford University Press, 1965), p. 379.

10. *Constitution on the Sacred Liturgy,* paragraph 67.

11. "Christian Initiation of Adults: The Rites," in *Made, Not Born* (Notre Dame: University of Notre Dame Press, 1976), p. 118.

12. *The Church in the Power of the Spirit* (New York: Harper & Row, 1977), pp. 226-42.

13. *Doxology* (New York: Oxford University Press, 1980).

14. Karl Barth, *The Teaching of the Church Regarding Baptism* (London: SCM Press, 1948); Oscar Cullmann, *Baptism in the New Testament* (London: SCM Press, 1950).

15. Joachim Jeremias, *Infant Baptism in the First Four Centuries* (Philadelphia: The Westminster Press, 1961) and *The Origins of Infant Baptism* (Philadelphia: The Westminster Press, 1963); Kurt Aland, *Did the Early Church Baptize Infants?* (London: SCM Press, 1963).

16. (Grand Rapids: Wm. B. Eerdmans Publishing Co., 1978).

17. (Grand Rapids: Wm. B. Eerdmans Publishing Co., 1979).

18. *The Shape of Baptism* (New York: Pueblo Publishing Co., 1978), p. 110.

19. *The Sacraments: Readings in Contemporary Theology* (New York: Alba House, 1981), pp. 95-103.

20. *Instruction on Infant Baptism* (Vatican City: Polyglot, 1980).

21. *Lutheran Book of Worship* (Minneapolis: Augsburg Publishing House, 1978), pp. 308-12; 324-27; *Book of Common Prayer* (New York: Church Hymnal

Corp., 1979), pp. 299-314; *We Gather Together* (Nashville: Abingdon Press, 1980), pp. 13-17.

22. For a short history of confirmation cf. my *Introduction to Christian Worship* (Nashville: Abingdon Press, 1980), pp. 181-87.

23. Cf. Kavanagh, *The Shape of Baptism*, for a full interpretation.

3. The Gift of Eucharist

1. *Eucharistic Words of Jesus* (New York: Charles Scribner's Sons, 1966), pp. 106-37.

2. English translation, A. G. Hebert (London: S.P.C.K., 1930).

3. Cf. especially on this: Thomas Talley, "The Eucharistic Prayer of the Ancient Church According to Recent Research: Results and Reflections," *Studia Liturgica* XI (3/4, 1976), 138-58; also Louis Ligier, "The Origins of the Eucharistic Prayer," trans. Geoffrey Wainwright, *Studia Liturgica* IX (4, 1973), 161-85, also (with caution) Louis Bouyer, *Eucharist* (Notre Dame, Ind.: University of Notre Dame Press, 1968).

4. *Early Christian Fathers*, edited by Cyril Richardson (Philadelphia: The Westminster Press, 1953), p. 175.

5. "First Apology," *Early Christian Fathers*, p. 287.

6. Joseph Keenan, "The Importance of the Creation Motif in a Eucharistic Prayer," *Worship*, LIII (July, 1979), 341-56.

7. Cf. Robert Daly, *Christian Sacrifice* (Washington: Catholic University of America Press, 1978), Robert Daly, *The Origins of the Christian Doctrine of Sacrifice* (Philadelphia: Fortress Press, 1978).

8. Cf. Gustaf Aulén, *Eucharist and Sacrifice* (Philadelphia: Fortress Press, 1958), pp. 146-50.

9. *Eucharistic Words of Jesus*, pp. 248-55.

10. Par. 7.

11. Edward Schillebeeckx, *Eucharist* (New York: Sheed & Ward, 1968).

12. See R. G. Jasper and G. J. Cuming, eds. *Prayers of the Eucharist: Early and Reformed*, 2d ed. (New York: Oxford University Press, 1980), p. 21 for convenient access to the text. Bernard Botte, *La Tradition apostolique de Saint Hippolyte* (Münster: Aschendorffsche, 1963) indicates problems with the epiclesis in Hippolytus, but retains it, p. 17 n.

13. Frank Cross, ed. *St. Cyril of Jerusalem's Lectures on the Christian Sacraments* (London: S.P.C.K., 1960), p. 74.

14. A. John McKenna, *Eucharist and Holy Spirit* (London: Alcuin Club, 1975).

15. Geoffrey Wainwright, *Eucharist and Eschatology* (New York: Oxford University Press, 1981) for a classic treatment of this theme.

16. Letter dated Sept. 10, 1784 and bound in *The Sunday Service of the Methodists in North America* (London: 1784).

17. Andrew D. Ciferni, "The Paschal Mystery: In the Eucharist and the Hours," *Liturgy*, XXII (Nov., 1977), p. 17.

18. An outstanding development of these possibilities occurs in *Praise God in Song* by John Allyn Melloh and William G. Storey (Chicago: G. I. A. Publications, 1979).

19. *The Word in Worship* (Nashville: Abingdon Press, 1981), pp. 65-77.

20. Cf. Reginald Fuller, *What Is Liturgical Preaching?* (London: SCM Press, 1957).

21. The best study remains Urban T. Holmes', *Young Children and the Eucharist*, rev. ed. (New York: The Seabury Press, 1982).

22. Cf. John D. C. Fisher, *Christian Initiation* (London: S.P.C.K., 1965), pp. 101-8.

23. For text cf. *The Rites* (New York: Pueblo Publishing Co., 1976), pp. 40-106.

24. *Institutes*, IV, xvii, 7, p. 1367.

4. Apostolic and Natural Sacraments

1. For historical development of these rites cf. my *Introduction to Christian Worship*, esp. "Initiation and Reconciliation," pp. 171-202 and "Passages," pp. 237-71, plus attendant notes.

2. Text in Elizabeth Frances Rogers, ed. *Peter Lombard and the Sacramental System* (Merrick, N.Y.: Richwood Publishing Co., 1976), IV, ii, 1; p. 85.

3. Mandate IV, iii, 6. Trans. Kirsopp Lake, *The Apostolic Fathers* (Cambridge, Mass.: Harvard University Press, 1965), II, 85.

4. Cf. *The Rites*, pp. 311-79.

5. A good resource from the Church of the Brethren, which has practiced anointing for the sick for centuries, is *Pastor's Manual* (Elgin, Ill.: Brethren Press, 1978), pp. 63-71.

6. Possible parallels in the Jewish recognition of religious authorities are explored by Lawrence A. Hoffman, "Jewish Ordination on the Eve of Christianity," *Studia Liturgica* XIII, 2-4, (1979), 11-41. This entire issue is a collection of papers on ordination rites.

7. "Letter to the Smyrnaeans," 8:1, *Early Christian Fathers*, p. 115.

8. Cf. Hervé-Marie Legrand, "The Presidency of the Eucharist According to the Ancient Tradition," *Worship*, LIII (Sept., 1979), 413-38.

9. Cf. Helmut Richard Niebuhr, *The Purpose of the Church and Its Ministry* (New York: Harper & Brothers, 1956), p. 64.

10. Cf. Edward Schillebeeckx, *Marriage: Human Reality and Saving Mystery* (New York: Sheed & Ward, 1965). Also, in response, Paul F. Palmer, "Christian Marriage: Contract or Covenant?" *Theological Studies* (Dec., 1972), pp. 617-65.

11. Cf. Geoffrey Rowell, *The Liturgy of Christian Burial* (London: S.P.C.K., 1977), pp. 1-98, and Richard Rutherford, *The Death of a Christian* (New York: Pueblo Pubishing Co., 1980), pp. 3-107.

12. A good outline of the grief process appears in A *Service of Death and Resurrection* (Nashville: Abingdon Press, 1979), pp. 20-34.

5. Sacraments and Justice

1. (Boston: Pilgrim, 1910.) Cf. Horton M. Davies, "The Expression of the Social Gospel in Worship," *Studia Liturgica*, II (September, 1963), 174-92.

2. Acquinas, *Summa Theologica* II/II, q. 58, a. 1 (New York: Benziger Brothers, 1947), II, 1435.

3. *Galatians*, Hermeneia Commentary (Philadelphia: Fortress Press, 1979), p. 184.

4. *Baptism in the New Testament* (London: SCM Press, 1950), p. 19.

5. *Ibid.*, p. 20. Italics in original.

6. *The Shape of Baptism* (New York: Pueblo Publishing Co., 1978), p. 188.

7. "On Baptism," ch. 17. *Ante-Nicene Fathers* (New York: Charles Scribner's Sons, 1899), III, 678-79.

8. *We Gather Together* (Nashville: The United Methodist Publishing House, 1980), p. 11.

9. *Worship: Its Theology and Practice* (New York: Oxford University Press, 1965), pp. 62-68.

10. *The Eucharist and Human Liberation* (Maryknoll, N.Y.: Orbis Books, 1979).

6. The Reform of Sacramental Practice

1. *Pastoral Liturgy* (London: Challoner, 1963), p. 380.
2. For a fuller treatment of these, see the author's *New Forms of Worship* (Nashville: Abingdon Press, 1971), chaps. 1-3.
3. Cf. George S. Worgul, Jr., *From Magic to Metaphor* (New York: Paulist Press, 1980), pp. 47-120.

For Further Reading ———°

1. The Humanity of the Sacraments

Baillie, Donald. *Theology of the Sacraments.* New York: Scribner's, 1957.

Casel, Odo. *The Mystery of Christian Worship.* Ed. by Burkhard Neunheuser and trans. by I. T. Hale. Westminster, Md.: Newman Press, 1962.

Cooke, Bernard J. *Christian Sacraments and Christian Personality.* New York: Holt, Rinehart and Winston, 1965.

Davies, J. G., ed. *Westminster Dictionary of Worship.* Philadelphia: The Westminster Press, 1979.

Eigo, Francis A., ed. *The Sacraments: God's Love and Mercy Actualized.* Villanova, Pa.: Villanova University Press, 1979.

Gelpi, Donald L. *Charism and Sacrament.* New York: Paulist Press, 1976.

Haring, Bernard. *The Sacraments and Your Everyday Life.* Liguori, Mo.: Ligouri Publications, 1976.

Hatchett, Marion Joseph. *Sanctifying Life, Time, and Space.* New York: Seabury Press, 1976.

Hellwig, Monika. *The Meaning of the Sacraments.* Dayton: Pflaum/Standard, 1972.

Jenson, Robert W. *Visible Words: The Practice and Interpretation of Christian Sacraments.* Philadelphia: Fortress Press, 1978.

Jones, Cheslyn, Wainwright, Geoffrey, and Yarnold, Edward, eds. *The Study of Liturgy.* New York: Oxford University Press, 1978.

Leeming, Bernard. *Principles of Sacramental Theology.* London: Longmans Green Ltd., 1960.

McBrien, Richard P. *Catholicism.* Minneapolis: Winston Press Inc., 1980. 2 vols.

Powers, Joseph M. *Spirit and Sacrament: The Humanizing Experience.* New York: The Seabury Press, Inc., 1973.

Rahner, Karl. *The Church and the Sacraments*. New York: Herder & Herder, 1963.

Saliers, Don E. *The Soul in Paraphrase: Prayer and the Religious Affections*. New York: Seabury Press, 1980.

Schmemann, Alexander. *Introduction to Liturgical Theology*. Portland, Maine: American Orthodox Press, 1970.

Shaughnessy, James, ed. *The Roots of Ritual*. Grand Rapids: Wm. B. Eerdmans Publishing Co., 1973.

Taylor, Michael J., ed. *The Sacraments: Readings in Contemporary Theology*. Staten Island, N.Y.: Alba House, 1981.

Vaillancourt, Raymond. *Toward a Renewal of Sacramental Theology*. Collegeville, Minn.: Liturgical Press, 1979.

White, James F. *Christian Worship in Transition*. Nashville: Abingdon Press, 1976.

Worden, Thomas, ed. *Sacraments in Scripture, A Symposium*. London: Geoffrey Chapman, 1966.

Worgul, George S. *From Magic to Metaphor*. New York: Paulist Press, 1980.

2. The Gift of Baptism

Beasley-Murray, G. R. *Baptism in the New Testament*. New York: St. Martins Press, 1961. London: Macmillan & Co., 1962.

Brand, Eugene L. *Baptism: A Pastoral Perspective*. Minneapolis: Augsburg Publishing House, 1975.

Cully, Kendig Brubaker, ed. *Confirmation: History, Doctrine, and Practice*. Greenwich, Conn.: The Seabury Press, Inc., 1962.

Davies, J. G. *The Architectural Setting for Baptism*. London: Barrie and Rockliff, 1962.

Eliade, Mircea. *Rites and Symbols of Initiation; The Mysteries of Birth and Re-birth*. New York: Harper & Row, 1965.

Fisher, John D. C. *Christian Initiation: Baptism in the Medieval West*. London: S.P.C.K., 1965.

———. *Christian Initiation: The Reformation Period*. London: S.P.C.K., 1970.

———. *Confirmation Then and Now*. London: S.P.C.K., 1978.

George, A. et al. *Baptism in the New Testament*. Baltimore: Helicon Press, 1964.

Gilmore, Alec, ed. *Christian Baptism*. Valley Forge, Pa.: Judson Press, 1959.

Kavanagh, Aidan. *The Shape of Baptism: The Rite of Christian Initiation*. New York: Pueblo Publishing Co., 1978.

Made, Not Born. Notre Dame: University of Notre Dame Press, 1976.

Mitchell, Leonel L. *Baptismal Anointing*. Notre Dame, Ind.: University of Notre Dame Press, 1977.

Neunheuser, Burkhard. *Baptism and Confirmation*. New York: Herder & Herder, 1964.

Riley, Hugh. *Christian Initiation*. (Studies in Christian Antiquity: vol. 17) Washington: The Catholic University of America Press, 1974.

Rite of Penance: Commentaries. Washington: Liturgical Conference, 1975-77. 3 vols.

Schnackenburg, Rudolf. *Baptism in the Thought of St. Paul*. New York: Herder and Herder, 1964.

Searle, Mark. *Christening: The Making of Christians*. Collegeville, Minn.: The Liturgical Press, 1980.

Stookey, Laurence H. *Baptism: Christ's Act in the Church*. Nashville: Abingdon Press, 1982.

Wainwright, Geoffrey. *Christian Initiation*. London: Lutterworth Press, 1969.

Whitaker, E. C. *Documents of the Baptismal Liturgy*. London: S.P.C.K., 1970.

3. The Gift of Eucharist

Aulén, Gustaf. *Eucharist and Sacrifice*. Philadelphia: Muhlenberg Press, 1958.

Bouyer, Louis. *Eucharist: Theology and Spirituality of the Eucharistic Prayer*. Notre Dame, Ind.: University of Notre Dame Press, 1968.

Brilioth, Yngve Torgny. *Eucharistic Faith and Practice*. Trans. by A. G. Hebert. New York and Toronto: Macmillan, 1930.

Buxton, R. F. *Eucharist and Institution Narrative: A Study in the Roman and Anglican Traditions of the Eucharist from the Eighth to the Twentieth Centuries*. London: Alcuin Club, 1976.

Church of England Doctrine Commission. *Thinking about the Eucharist*. London: SCM Press, 1972.

Clements, Ronald E., et al. *Eucharistic Theology Then and Now*. London: S.P.C.K., 1968. Naperville, Ill.: Alec R. Allenson, 1968.

COCU. *Word, Bread, Cup*. Cincinnati: Forward Movement, 1978.

Daly, Robert. *Christian Sacrifice* (Studies in Christian Antiquity; vol. 18). Washington: The Catholic University of America Press, 1978.

Delorme, J. H., et al. *The Eucharist in the New Testament*. Baltimore: Helicon, 1964.

Dix, Gregory. *The Shape of the Liturgy*. Westminster, Eng.: Dacre, 1945.

Emminghaus, Johannes H. *The Eucharist: Essence, Form, Celebration*. Collegeville, Minn.: The Liturgical Press, 1978.

Guzie, Tad W. *Jesus and the Eucharist*. New York: Paulist Press, 1974.

Jasper, R. C. D., ed. *The Eucharist Today*. London: S.P.C.K., 1974.

Jasper, R. C. D. and Cuming, G. J., eds. *Prayers of the Eucharist: Early and Reformed*. 2nd ed. New York: Oxford University Press, 1980.

Jeremias, Joachim. *Eucharistic Words of Jesus*. Philadelphia: Fortress Press, 1977.

Jungmann, Josef. *The Early Liturgy*. Trans. Francis A. Brunner. Liturgical Studies, vol. 6. Notre Dame, Ind.: University of Notre Dame Press, 1959.

―――. *The Mass of the Roman Rite*. New York: Benziger Brothers, 1950, 1951, 1952, 1955, 2 vols.

Klauser, Theodor. *A Short History of the Western Liturgy*. London: Oxford University Press, 1969.

Marshall, I. Howard. *Last Supper and Lord's Supper*. Grand Rapids: Wm. B. Eerdmans Publishing Co., 1981.

Martimort, A. G. *The Church at Prayer: The Eucharist*. New York: Herder and Herder, 1968.

McKenna, John. *Eucharist and Holy Spirit: The Eucharistic Epiclesis in Twentieth Century Theology (1900-1966)*. London: Alcuin Club, 1975.

Powers, J. M. *Eucharistic Theology*. New York: Herder & Herder, 1967.

Ratcliff, E. C. *Liturgical Studies*. London: S.P.C.K., 1976.

Rordorf, Willy, et al. *The Eucharist of the Early Christians*. New York: Pueblo Publishing Co., 1978.

Ryan, John Barry. *The Eucharistic Prayer*. New York: Paulist Press, 1974.

Schillebeeckx, Edward. *The Eucharist*. New York: Sheed & Ward, 1968.

Spinks, Bryan, ed. *The Sacrifice of Praise: Studies on the Themes of Thanksgiving and Redemption in the Central Prayers of the Eucharistic and Baptismal Liturgies*. Rome: Edizioni Liturgiche, 1981.

Vagaggini, C. *The Canon of the Mass and Liturgical Reform*. London: Geoffrey Chapman, 1967.

Wainwright, Geoffrey. *Eucharist and Eschatology*. New York: Oxford University Press, 1981.

Watkins, Keith. *The Feast of Joy*. St. Louis: Bethany Press, 1977.

4. Apostolic and Natural Sacraments

Anderson, Ray S., ed. *Theological Foundations for Ministry*. Grand Rapids: Wm. B. Eerdmans Publishing Co., 1978.

Bradshaw, Paul F. *The Anglican Ordinal*. London: S.P.C.K., 1971.

Cooke, Bernard. *Ministry to Word and Sacraments: History and Theology*. Philadelphia: Fortress Press, 1980.

Cope, Gilbert, ed. *Dying, Death, and Disposal*. London: S.P.C.K., 1970.

Dwyer, Walter W. *The Churches' Handbook for Spiritual Healing*. New York: Ascension Press, 1962.

Irion, Paul E. *The Funeral: Vestige or Value?* Nashville: Abingdon Press, 1966.

Jackson, Edgar N. *The Christian Funeral*. New York: Channel Press, 1966. Meredith, 1966.

Kelsey, Morton T. *Healing and Christianity*. New York: Harper & Row, 1973.

Kilmartin, Edward J. *Church, Eucharist, and Priesthood*. New York: Paulist Press, 1981.

Knauber, Adolf. *Pastoral Theology of the Anointing of the Sick*. Collegeville, Minn.: The Liturgical Press, 1975.

McNeill, John T. *A History of the Cure of Souls*. New York: Harper & Row, 1977.

Porter, H. Boone. *Ordination Prayers of the Ancient Western Churches*. Naperville, Ill.: Alec R. Anderson, 1967.

Power, David, and Maldonado, Luis, eds. *Liturgy and Human Passage*. New York: Seabury Press, 1979.

Prayer Book Studies #20. *The Ordination of Bishops, Priests, and Deacons*. New York: Church Hymnal Corporation, 1970.

Rowell, Geoffrey. *The Liturgy of Christian Burial*. London: S.P.C.K., 1977.

Rutherford, Richard. *The Death of a Christian: The Rite of Funerals*. New York: Pueblo Publishing Co., 1980.

Schillebeeckx, Edward. *Marriage: Human Reality and Saving Mystery*. New York: Sheed & Ward, 1965.

van Gennep, Arnold. *Rites of Passage*. London: Routledge & Kegan Paul, 1960.

Willimon, William H. *Worship As Pastoral Care*. Nashville: Abingdon Press, 1979.

5. Sacraments and Justice

Avila, Rafael. *Worship and Politics*. Trans. by Alan Neely. Maryknoll, N.Y.: Orbis Books, 1981.

Balasuriya, Tissa. *The Eucharist and Human Liberation*. Maryknoll, N.Y.: Orbis Books, 1979.

Bonino, Jose Miguez. *Doing Theology in a Revolutionary Situation*. Philadelphia: Fortress Press, 1975.

Cone, James H. *Black Theology and Black Power*. New York: The Seabury Press, 1969.

Emswiler, Sharon Neufer and Emswiler, Tom. *Wholeness in Worship*. San Francisco: Harper & Row, 1980.

Gutiérrez, Gustavo. *A Theology of Liberation*. Maryknoll, N.Y.: Orbis Books, 1973.

Hill, Edmund. *Prayer, Praise, and Politics*. London: Sheed & Ward, 1973.

Ogden, Schubert M. *Faith and Freedom: Toward a Theology of Liberation*. Nashville: Abingdon Press, 1979.

Sawicki, Marianne. *Faith and Sexism*. New York: The Seabury Press, 1979.

Schmidt, Herman and Power, David, eds. *Politics and Liturgy*. Concilium vol. 92. New York: The Crossroad Publishing Co., 1974.

Segundo, Juan Luis. *The Sacraments Today*. Trans. by John Drury. Maryknoll, N.Y.: Orbis Books, 1974.

Watkins, Keith. *Faithful & Fair: Transcending Sexist Language in Worship*. Nashville: Abingdon Press, 1981.

7. The Reform of Sacramental Practice

Hanson, Anthony. *Church, Sacraments and Ministry*. London: Mowbrays, 1975.

Hardin, H. Grady. *The Leadership of Worship*. Nashville: Abingdon Press, 1980.

Hovda, Robert W. *Strong, Loving & Wise: Presiding in Liturgy*. Washington: Liturgical Conference, 1976.

Mitchell, Leonel. *Liturgical Change: How Much Do We Need?* New York: The Seabury Press, 1975.

Senn, Frank. *The Pastor As Worship Leader: A Manual for Corporate Worship*. Minneapolis, Minn.: Augsburg Publishing House, 1977.

White, James F. *New Forms of Worship*. Nashville: Abingdon Press, 1971.

Winstone, Harold, ed. *Pastoral Liturgy: A Symposium*. London: Collins, 1975.

Word and Table. Rev. ed. Nashville: Abingdon Press, 1980.

Index

153